*When dost thou
bring out a lamp
**then** to hide it away
beneath bed or bowl?*

*Wouldst thou not first
place it up on a stand
so the flames can be
shared all around?*

JESUS OF NAZARETH

BOOK of JESUS - A UNIFIED
GOSPEL IN ENGLISH VERSE (2025)
Translation © E. d'Araille, 2021-2024.
Vol. #1 of a 3-volume set © LTB™, 2024.
First published in the *Deluxe Int'l Library
Edition* (Hbk) by LIVING TIME™ BOOKS, 2025.

The right of Edouard d'Araille to be identified as author
of this translation is asserted by him in accordance with
the *'Copyright, Designs and Patents Act 1988'* (UK Law).

ALL RIGHTS RESERVED. No portion of this publication may be
reproduced, stored in a retrieval system, or be transmitted in
any form, or by any means - electronic, mechanical, photocopying,
recording or otherwise - without having the previous permission of
the publisher of this work, LIVING TIME ™ BOOKS. Nor may any part
of this publication be otherwise circulated in any form of binding
or cover other than that in which it is published and without all
similar conditions being imposed on the subsequent publisher.
All forms of piracy of this verse translation, **BOOK of JESUS**,
shall be pursued with litigation - civil and/or criminal -
in all international jurisdictions which so permit.

A CIP (Cataloguing in Publication) Data Record
for this title is available from *The British Library*.

ISBN 978-1-908936-61-5

Afterword, *'Apologia Poetæ:
THE POET'S APOLOGY'* ©
Edouard d'Araille 2024.

LIVING TIME™ BOOKS
livingtimebooks.com

# BOOK of JESUS

A UNIFIED GOSPEL
IN ENGLISH VERSE

VOLUME I

# BOOK of JESUS

## A UNIFIED GOSPEL IN ENGLISH VERSE

### VOLUME I

*The One who
comes **after** me
comes **above** me
because He came
**before** me —*

JOHN THE BAPTIST

*Composed by*

## Edouard d'Araille

*and based entirely upon the complete
texts of the four canonical gospels -
of Matthew, Mark, Luke & John*

# BOOK of JESUS

A UNIFIED GOSPEL IN ENGLISH VERSE

# PAGEFINDER

BOOK of JESUS — PUBLISHER'S PREFACE .................................................. ix

TRANSLATION & RESEARCH ACKNOWLEDGEMENTS .................................. x

A NOTE UPON CAPITALIZATION ............................................................... xi

## BOOK of JESUS

A UNIFIED GOSPEL
IN ENGLISH VERSE

*'HOW MANY ARE THE AUTHORS'* ................. *unnumbered*

PROLOGUS: *ANTE OMNIA* ........................................ 1

## 0. BEFORE THE BEGINNING

*1.* THE VISION OF ZECHARIAH ............................................................. 11

*2.* THE BETROTHED ............................................................................. 18

*3.* A VIRGIN'S VISITATION .................................................................... 20

*4.* THE FIRST DREAM OF JOSEPH ......................................................... 24

*5.* A PROPHET'S WORDS FULFILLED .................................................... 25

*6.* '*AS THE LORD COMMANDS*' ............................................................. 26

*7.* "BLESSÈD ART THOU" ...................................................................... 27

*8.* THE SONG OF MARY ........................................................................ 29

*9.* '*HIS NAME IS JOHN*' ........................................................................ 31

*10.* THE SONG OF ZECHARIAH ............................................................. 34

# I. A NEW LIFE

*11.* A CENSUS FOR CÆSAR ........................................................... 38

*12.* IN THE TOWN OF DAVID .......................................................... 40

*13.* SHEPHERDS PAY HOMAGE ..................................................... 45

*14. "WHERE IS THE NEW KING?"* ..................................................... 48

*15.* THREE MAGI BRING TRIBUTES ................................................. 52

*16.* A TIME FOR PURIFICATION ..................................................... 54

*17.* SIMEON'S BLESSING ............................................................... 56

*18.* ANNA, THE PROPHETESS ........................................................ 59

*19.* A DREAM OF EGYPT ................................................................ 61

*20.* HEROD'S VENOM ..................................................................... 62

*21.* A DREAM IN EGYPT ................................................................. 65

*22.* 'A NAZARENE' .......................................................................... 68

*23.* JESUS IS LOST .......................................................................... 70

*24. "IN MY FATHER'S HOUSE"* ......................................................... 72

*25.* OBEDIENCE AND WISDOM ...................................................... 75

# II. 'THE ANOINTED ONE'

*26.* THE WORD OF GOD ................................................................. 78

*27. "MAKE READY THE WAY"* .......................................................... 80

*28.* *'THE LAMB OF GOD'* .................................................................. 91

*29.* FOLLOWERS OF JESUS .............................................................. 97

*30.* A WEDDING MIRACLE ............................................................. 102

# III. A NEW MESSAGE

*31.* TEMPTATIONS OF SATAN ....................................................... 108

*32.* "DESTROY THIS TEMPLE, I WILL RAISE IT UP!" ................. 114

*33.* TO BE BORN ANEW .................................................................. 120

*34.* JESUS BAPTIZING ..................................................................... 126

*35.* THE WELL OF LIFE ETERNAL ................................................. 131

*36.* THE HARVEST OF ETERNAL LIFE ......................................... 140

*37.* NEW BELIEVERS ....................................................................... 144

*38.* THE BAPTIST IMPRISONED .................................................... 146

*39.* "REPENT, THE KINGDOM OF GOD IS NIGH!" ..................... 149

*40.* "THY SON SHALL LIVE" ......................................................... 151

*41.* A RABBI MOST UNWELCOME ............................................... 156

*42.* "EVEN DEMONS OBEY HIM!" ................................................ 164

*43.* A DISCIPLE'S MOTHER CURED ............................................. 168

*44.* THE NEWS OF ALL GALILEE .................................................. 170

*45.* A MOMENT OF SOLITUDE ...................................................... 173

## IV. <u>NEW TEACHINGS</u>

*46.* "BLESSÈD ARE YE" ............................................................ 177

*47.* "YET WOE TO YE ALL" ...................................................... 182

*48.* SALT OF THE EARTH ....................................................... 183

*49.* "YOU ARE THE LIGHT OF THE WORLD" ........................ 184

*50.* THE LAW OF THE KINGDOM ........................................... 189

*51.* 'DO NO MURDER' ............................................................. 191

*52.* REGARDING ADULTERY ................................................. 193

*53.* A WORD ON DIVORCE .................................................... 195

*54.* "SWEAR NO OATHS" ....................................................... 196

*55.* 'AN EYE FOR AN EYE'? .................................................... 198

*56.* "LOVE THY ENEMIES" ..................................................... 200

*57.* THE MEANING OF 'RIGHTEOUSNESS' .......................... 204

*58.* "OUR FATHER, WHO ART IN HEAVEN" ......................... 206

*59.* "IN SECRET, YOU ARE SEEN" ........................................ 210

*60.* TREASURES IN HEAVEN ................................................ 212

*61.* "BEWARE DARKNESS WITHIN" ..................................... 213

*62.* GOD AND MAMMON ....................................................... 214

*63.* WISDOM FOR TOMORROW ........................................... 215

*64.* 'JUDGE AND BE JUDGED' .............................................. 219

65. BLIND LEADING BLIND .................................................. 222

66. "ASK AND IT SHALL BE GIVEN TO YOU" ..................... 223

67. 'NARROW IS THE GATE' ............................................. 228

68. TRUE AND FALSE PROPHETS ..................................... 229

69. WHAT THE MOUTH SPEAKS ....................................... 231

70. TRUE AND FALSE DISCIPLES ...................................... 232

71. 'LIKE A HOUSE BUILT ON ROCK' ............................... 234

72. "TELL NO-ONE OF THIS" ............................................ 236

# V. A NEW CALLING

73. A SIGN OF FISH ......................................................... 241

74. THE MIRACLE OF FORGIVENESS ................................ 247

75. DINING WITH SINNERS ............................................ 254

76. A QUESTION OF FASTING ........................................ 258

77. 'SOMEWHERE GREATER THAN A TEMPLE' ................ 261

78. "STRETCH OUT THY HAND!" ..................................... 265

79. A MULTIPLICATION OF FOLLOWERS ........................ 270

80. 'MY SPIRIT UPON HIM' ............................................ 273

81. "I NAME YE TWELVE" ............................................... 274

82. DANCING WITH THE DEVIL ..................................... 276

83. A NOTE UPON DEMONS AND A BLESSING ............... 283

84. *"MY MOTHER AND MY BROTHERS"* .............................................. 285

85. IN ALL ISRAEL KNOWN ................................................................ 287

# VI. HEALING

86. THE FAITH OF A ROMAN ............................................................. 291

87. FROM DEATH TO LIFE ................................................................. 296

88. THE PRICE OF FAITH .................................................................... 298

89. *"EVEN THE WINDS AND WAVES"* ............................................. 300

90. *"DEMONS BEGONE!"* ................................................................. 304

91. SICKNESS UNTO DEATH ............................................................. 316

92. ALL ADVERSITIES ARE OVERCOME ........................................ 323

93. *"ARE YOU THE ONE?"* ................................................................ 326

94. ANOINTED WITH TEARS ............................................................ 333

95. HEALERS FOR THE KINGDOM .................................................. 337

96. HEALING UPON A DAY OF REST .............................................. 339

97. *"WHAT THE FATHER DOES, THE SON DOES ALSO"* ............ 342

THE TASK IS THE TESTIMONY ......................................................... 347

    ✻        ✻        ✻        ✻        ✻

*Apologia Poetæ* — THE POET'S APOLOGY — *by* EDOUARD d'ARAILLE ................ 353

~ *YESHUA HAMASHIACH* ~

JESUS 'THE ANOINTED ONE'

— BORN BETHLEHEM 4 BCE —

> *I say that ye shall earn one hundred times more — inherit* **the Life Eternal**
>
> MANY NOW FIRST
> WILL BE LAST —
> AND NOW LAST
> SHALL BE FIRST!
>
> **JESUS OF NAZARETH**

## BOOK of JESUS
### PUBLISHER'S PREFACE

IT WAS FIRST IN 2020 that the publishers - LIVING TIME™ BOOKS - set in motion the long-term project that would ultimately become ***Book of Jesus*** — which is a new translation of the canonical gospels entirely into English verse, with the intent of reflecting every single detail in the evangelists' texts whilst ensuring that the events of Jesus's life are told in a single, continuous, predominantly chronological narrative. It has taken till January of 2025 for this project to come to fruition with the release of the present publication - volume one of the three-part set entitled '***Book of Jesus**: A Unified Gospel in English Verse*'. As a whole, this work presents the gospel story as a series of around 300 chapters of poetry in the span of over a thousand pages of verse, researched and composed by contemporary English language poet Edouard d'Araille. Previous to this, all that had been released of his new translation of the New Testament gospels was the limited edition volume '*Birth of Jesus: Nativity and Anointment*', which first appeared in December of 2023.

One core aim of the project was to use poetry in the most natural way so as to express the words and events of the canon gospels as accurately as possible, never losing touch with their language and detail, all the time endeavoring to represent every single incident and conversation from the life of Jesus — contained in the gospels — as faithfully as possible. It is important to emphasize that the '***Book of Jesus***' is not a compendium of poems inspired by chapters from the evangelists or an attempt at putting the four gospels into rhyme, or even an exercise in re-writing the gospels liberally in verse. No, the aim has always been the same, from the very start, which has been for the poet - functioning as translator - to transform the core gospel texts, written for the most part in prose, into a unified poetic whole that does not harmfully distort any of the gospels' narratives, hopefully making them resonate in new ways with English readers. As any cursory examination of this volume will reveal, the poet at no point descends into childish rhythms and rhymes, restrictive structures like the sonnet or sestina, or any fixed meter throughout - such as the alexandrine or iambic pentameter.

On the contrary, his poetry appears to use the simplest forms possible so as to adapt each chapter to its content and sequence, selecting the words and phrases that most effectively turn the Koine Greek of the original evangelists into English that rings true for modern readers. The publishers have demanded of the poet that he take into account every single sentence of each one of the four gospels, channeling all of the incidents and language of the evangelists into a single, unified poetic work. Surpsisingly, although there is a long history of 'Gospel Harmonies' dating back to the 2nd Century ACE, rarely were they done in verse, though there are good reasons to favor poetry over prose, which Edouard d'Araille discusses in his afterword, '*Apologia Poetæ*'.

In that essay, the composer of this translation explains how he came to the tasks of researching and writing the unified verse translation that is presented in the three volumes of '**Book of Jesus**', touching upon the thinking processes behind the poetry and unique challenges faced in attempting to unify the four separate gospels into a single poetic work. Volume II of '**Book of Jesus**' is being released in December 2025, continuing directly from where the gospel narrative ends in this volume: Jesus is followed into the heart of his ministry of God's 'Good News'. The third and final volume of '**Book of Jesus**' is releasing in Easter 2026.

*Algernon P. Smith* ANCIENT SCRIPTURES EDITOR, LTB™ — January 1st 2025

## TRANSLATION & RESEARCH
## ACKNOWLEDGEMENTS

IN SUCH AN ABBREVIATED FORM as this, it is only possible to faintly hint towards the many debts of knowledge that are owed to an extremely wide range of texts and authors: the best-preserved source texts in the original Koine Greek, in excess of fifty New Testament translations of the Bible gospels, the non-canonical gospels (helpful to issues of chronology and in other ways), the body of 'Gospel Harmonies' that have been produced since the *Diatesseron* of Tatian (circa 160 ACE) and the absolutely overwhelming wealth of scriptural scholarship that has amassed over nearly two millennia since the gospels first appeared. The voices of Irenaeus, St. Augustine and Thomas Aquinas, of Friedrich Schleiermacher, Søren Kierkegaard, Albert Schweitzer, William Barclay, Karl Barth, Gerd Lüdemann and William Lane Craig — these few represent only the tiniest chorus of those whose researches on translation, interpretation *et al.* have been considered during the convergence of the four gospel texts into this unified poetic work, however perilous may be the performance of such a task. Regarding the present volume in the series, it presents the openings stages of Jesus of Nazareth's life-story: his birth and childhood, his anointing by John the Baptist, the commencement of his teaching, the calling of his apostles and the first healings and wonders that are reported of him. By the end of this part we have arrived at the core of his ministry and he has announced much about the purpose of his actions. All errors of interpretation (that I have undoubtedly committed) in the composition of this work are due *to my self only* and cannot be blamed on any of the bible scholars to whom I have turned for alternative theories and opinions about all of the chapters and verses of the four gospels. It is a hope of the composer of this translation that it may offer new perspectives on the gospel story.

*Edouard d'Araille* — December 29th 2024

### A NOTE UPON CAPITALIZATION

Please take note that in some chapters Jesus of Nazareth has been referred to as 'He', 'Him' etc. - with a capitalized 'H' - while in other ones this is not the case. In those instances where such capitalization has occurred, the main reason for doing so has been to place emphasis upon *his person* - especially when another male pronoun has also been utilized in close textual proximity. It is the opinion of the translator that use of such capitalization may dispel confusion in a number of instances. It has **not** been done as an assertion of Jesus' divinity, *which is not a choice for the translator to make.* — Readers are free to interpret the capitalizations in the text however they wish. Christians and non-Christians will naturally tend to approach the text in alternative ways. Use of fully capitalized words has been done on numerous occasions for emphatic or dramatic effect, especially where it is believed that this will clarify the sense of the passage. Please note that the gospel sources are only indicated at the very end of each chapter, the names of the evangels being abbreviated as 'Mt' for Matthew, 'M' for Mark, 'L' for Luke and 'J' for John - followed by chapter and verse reference for the passage or passages forming the basis or the partial basis of that section. -

# BOOK of JESUS

## VOLUME I

> "*Verily, I say to thee:
> thine eyes will behold
> the Heavens open -
> Angels of God
> ascend and
> descend -
> the SON OF MAN
> thine eyes shall see!*"
>
> JESUS OF NAZARETH

*Composed by*

## Edouard d'Araille

*and based entirely upon the complete
text of the four canonical gospels -
of Matthew, Mark, Luke & John*

*To YOU,*
*O highest*
*friend of GOD*

*- **Theophilus** -*
*these words*
*I write. —*


(L 1:3)

*HOW MANY are the authors*

*who with words*

*have writ of*

*what occurred — of*

WHAT HAS BEEN FULFILLED?

*Verses that were passed down*

*to us — what eyes beheld*

*which* TESTIFIED

AS SERVANTS OF

THE **WORD.**

*In the steps of* YOUR *servants*
*I take up my pen and with words*
*delve back, on those moments reflect;*

*I strive to describe the events in order*
*that* **You** *may know the* REAL TRUTH
*— of all that has been learned.*

(L 1:1-4)

# BOOK of JESUS

*The LIGHT doth shine
in Darkness
and
by Darkness
**it shall not be drowned!***

A UNIFIED GOSPEL IN ENGLISH VERSE

# Prologus
ANTE OMNIA*

BEFORE
*All Else*
existed,

***Logos***
WAS

- the Word
which WAS
with GOD

and which
*itself*
WAS **GOD**.

Even since
the Birth
of Time

HE WAS
with
GOD.

\* 'Before Everything'

Through HIM,
a COSMOS
*came*
*to Being -*

without
HIM,
NOTHING
would become

— for HE
was L I F E,
illuminating
All who live.

*The LIGHT doth shine*
*in Darkness*
*and*
*by Darkness*
**it shall not be drowned!**

A man
named John
by GOD was sent

to testify about
*that Light.*

He came
as witness
to the Truth
so
*through him*
ALL MIGHT
**BELIEVE.**

This man
was not himself
*the LIGHT*

but came
*as witness to it -*

***a dawning Light***

now shines
upon
the World,
THAT ALL MAY SEE.

Through HIM,
a COSMOS
*came*
*to Being -*

without
HIM,
NOTHING
would become.

His being
grew up in
this World

yet although
He had come
from this World,

*it did not know Him.*

Unto this Earth
He came - His
Own World
*- but **by this
World, He was
barely welcomed.***

Yet
to those
who received
Him and

those
who believed
in His Holy Name,

*he granted the right
to be* CHILDREN
OF GOD -

children
not birthed
from a woman's
womb, nor by
will of man

- nor by
human
choice.

*His
children
were born
of GOD
alone.*

THE

WORD

BECAME

FLESH and

He founded

**His House**

*among us.*


We
have
opened
our eyes to
His GLORY —


*Pure Glory of a*

*Unique and*

*Solitary*

*Son.*

He
came from
the Father to us,

filled with Grace,

lit up by
Truth.

John, when
he spoke of Him,
testified thus:

*"for Here is
the One whom
I spoke of in
saying:*

**'The One who
comes after me
comes above me
because He came
before me.'** — "

Out

of HIS

PLENITUDE

all receive *grace*


- in the place

of GOD's

*grace,*

**which was**

**granted already.**


The *Law* - as we know

- it comes via Moses

yet Grace and Truth

are through Jesus


= THE CHRIST =

No human eyes

have *seen*

GOD

*ever*

*for* ONLY

*the unique,*

*the solitary*

One - who

is His Son

and GOD

Himself *in*

*union bound*

— REVEALS **HIM**.

(J 1:1-18)

# 0. <u>BEFORE THE BEGINNING</u>

*Devoid of form
was all — a Void —*

FACE OF NIGHT *was
upon the Abyss*

GENESIS 1:2

## 1. THE VISION OF ZECHARIAH

WHILE HEROD,
as King, ruled
in all of Judea,
*Zechariah* lived

— of the priestly
division of Abijah,
wed to *Elzbieta*,*
of Aaron's line.

Before God,
they were both
*so pure* - in His
eyes *so righteous*;

all His Laws
they honored —
commands obeyed —
of all blame they were free.

*But alas, of offspring
they were bereft.*

\* 'Elzbieta' - Elizabeth

- Elizabeth was
barren, she could
not conceive - both
her husband and she
so far gone in their years
*yet no child had they still.*

One day, while his order
performed sacred rites,
he was chosen at
random - as custom
dictates - holy incense to
burn in the House of God.

— Zechariah, he entered
the Temple of *YAHWEH,*
the hour approached that
the censer be lighted;

outside a congregation,
throngs awaited —
together were
joined in prayer.

That instant appeared
unto Zechariah
an angel of the Lord,
*standing right beside him*;

***there***, *at the right of
the altar - where
fragrance was burning -
HE looked straight at him.*

The priest was unsettled
- ***a fear*** *chilled his soul* -

yet the angel then spoke
to him, in these words:

*"Freeze not in terror,
dear Zechariah —
thy* SUPPLICATIONS,
*they have been heard.*

*Elizabeth - thy spouse -
shall bear a son to thee
and thou shalt call him
by the name of 'JOHN'.*

*The **Joy of Life** shall
HE be to you both and
to many HIS BIRTH — **it
shall bring jubilation**.*

*In the sight of the Lord
HE WILL HAVE GLORY
- nor liquor nor wine
will he ever imbibe;*

*'fore even this child
is out of the womb
- HIS SOUL IS INFUSED
WITH THE **HOLY SPIRIT**.*

*How many of Israel's
children shall **this one**
turn unto the Lord
— their God! —*

*To them he will
go with the soul
and the might of
ELIJAH before him.*

*Hearts of parents,
so hardened to Love, to
their children shall return;*

*those who have
disobeyed the Lord -* **to
the wisdom of HIS JUSTICE.**

*His actions will make
the people ready
for the* LORD."

Yet old Zechariah,
he voiced only
doubts, and
disbelief —

"*Of each word
that you say,*
**how can I be
so sure?** *- For
my body is ageing
and also my wife is
advanced in her years.*"

*Then to these words
did the angel respond:*

*"Gabriel am I
- **in the presence
of God I stand** and
to you have been sent
to share* SUCH GOOD NEWS.

*From this moment forth,*
THOU SHALT MAKE NOT
A SOUND — IN FACT
THOU WILT NOT SPEAK
TILL THE DAY THAT ALL THIS
HAS COME TO PASS - *for thou
didst not believe my words;*

*in good time, you will
see,* **they shall be
proven** TRUE*."*

While this happened,
the people outside who
were waiting ask: *"Why doth
he bide in the temple so long?"*

Yet when he emerged,
Zechariah SPOKE NOT
- people *sensed* he had
witnessed a vision inside.

He continued to beckon
to them with signs ***but
he could not utter
a single word.*** —

As soon as his duties had
been fulfilled,
the priest returned
to his home -

after that day
did Elizabeth duly
*conceive* - and five months
she remained all alone, thinking:

"*Thus hath the* LORD
*acted -* ***pitying me*** *- in
removing the shame that
had darkened my name.*"

(L 1:5-25)

## 2. **THE BETROTHED**

HERE FOLLOWETH
how those events
came to pass, that
the birth of *JESUS -
MESSIAH* - occurred:

The mother of Jesus,
named Mary, was
promised to Joseph who
from David hailed

— yet even before
they were joined as
one, she was found
to be pregnant - *by
the **Spirit**'s power*.

Joseph, faithful
to the LAW - and
not desirous of public
disgrace - was minded
to break off from
his betrothal.

\* \* \* \* \* \*

*At that time*
Elzbieta, with John,
was now six months
progressed *when*

God sent to Earth
GABRIEL - *angel* -
to Nazareth,
Galilee. —

He sent HIM to
Mary - *the virgin* -
whom Joseph had
pledged to wed.

(Mt 1:18-19 / L 1:26-27)

## 3. A VIRGIN'S VISITATION

WHEN GABRIEL
came unto Mary,
he said to her:

*"Greetings to thee -
thou who art so
highly blessed
among women —
the Lord is **with thee**."*

At these words
of the angel
was Mary
perturbed —
*wondering* quite
what the greeting meant.

However, he carried
on saying to her:

*"Be thou not afraid,
O Mary,
full favor hast
thou found with God.
A baby in thy womb shalt
thou conceive and to
this son give birth,
and name Him
as 'Jesus'.*

> "Upon THEE
> the HOLY SPIRIT
> shall descend; the might
> of the Lord on High shall cast
> His shadow upon **thee**"

*Great will He be  
and He shall be called  
The Son of the One Most High.*

*To Him, Lord God  
shall present the throne  
of David, His father on Earth*

*— over Jacob's sons and  
daughters, He will rule  
for ever more —  
His Kingdom never die."*

*"**But how can this be**,"  
Mary said to the angel,  
"**since I have never  
   lain with man?**"*

*To which Gabriel  
answered,  
saying:*

*"Upon thee  
the Holy Spirit  
shall descend; the might  
of the Lord on High shall cast  
His shadow upon **thee** - thus  
the Sacred One shall be  
born, to be known as  
the 'Son of God'."*

Then the angel
continued:

"*Elizabeth, thy kin,
herself will bear a child -
she who now is agèd and
has been called **barren** -
already today, she is
six months gone —*

*No Word of God
shall ever fail
to grow.*"


"***Handmaiden
of the Lord am I,***"

responded Mary:

"*Let every word
that* THOU *hast
said,* **thus** *be*
FULFILLED."


And at
that point
the angel left.


(L 1:27-38)

## 4. **THE FIRST DREAM OF JOSEPH**

AFTER JOSEPH
had dwelt on
these things
in his thoughts,

unto **him** came
an angel (the Lord's)
whilst dreaming,
and said to him:

*"Joseph - son of
David's House -
**Fear not** to make
Mary thy wife, to
bring her inside
thy home. For
that which is
inside her womb
takes its life from
the Holy Spirit.*

*A son, of Mary,
shall be born and
His name, IT SHALL BE
'JESUS' — for His nation
He brings from their
sins unto **Salvation**."*

(Mt 1:20-21)

# 5. A PROPHET'S WORDS FULFILLED

THUS DID
all this come to pass
that the words spake by God
through His prophet
should wholly be
fulfilled:

*"For*
*the Virgin*
*will then become*
*pregnant*
*and*
*then shall*
*give birth to a son*
*and to him*
*will*
*be*
*given*
*the name*
*'IMMANUEL'*
*—* **'God with Us'** *."*

(Mt 1:22-23)

## 6. 'AS THE LORD COMMANDS'

THUS
when Joseph
awakened, he did
what the Lord had
demanded
of him.

Mary
he took in
his house a*s*
*his spouse*,
yet
their union
would not be
consummated
till *after* the birth
of their **son** - and
to him he gave
the name
of 'Jesus'.

(Mt 1:24-25)

# 7. "BLESSÈD ART THOU"

THEN IT WAS
Mary made ready
and went with great haste
to a town in the hills
of Judea —

here did she
enter a home,
Zechariah's —
his wife Elizabeth
greeting her there.

The instant Elizabeth
heard Mary's voice
speak, the baby
leapt round in
her womb —

*she was filled
with the Holy Spirit*

— in voice
firm and strong
she proclaimed
unto Mary:

"— Blessèd art THOU
of all women and blessèd
the fruit that thy womb
shall bear.

Tell me, —
why am I so blessed
that the **Mother of the** L<small>ORD</small>
should come hither
to visit me?

— No sooner
than thou camest
near and the sound
of thy greeting was heard
in my ears - **then**
the infant leapt joyous
within me.

— Blessèd is she who
has fully believed that
the Lord would make good
on those promises that
He had made to us!"

(L 1:39-45)

## 8. THE SONG OF MARY

MARY THEN
proclaimed:

"*My soul sings its
glories to the* LORD,
*for my spirit rejoices
in all its joy, O* GOD
*-* **O MY SALVATION!**

*— For HE has
attended to one who
is modest in being
HIS* SERVANT.

*From this day forth,
all times and peoples
shall name me* '**blessèd**'
*for what* GOD ALMIGHTY
*performed through me.*

*Hallowed be* **His Name**
*— His Mercy reaches even
those who fear Him — from
one generation to the next.*

— *With His arms alone*
*He has mastered great feats;*
*those with naught but pride*
*in their innermost thoughts,*
*He has soon dispersed.*

*Kings has He thrown*
*from their thrones yet*
*the humble and meek -*
*He has hoisted on high.*

*Those who were famished,*
*He fed with His nourishment;*
*affluent ones He sent back to*
*their homes - empty-handed.*

*I*srael*, His servant, hath He*
*helped in many ways,*
*so mindful of her in*
*His* **mercy** *- to our*
*fathers,* A*braham*
*and his descendants,*
forever*, as was pledged."*

(L 1:46-55)

# 9. 'HIS NAME IS JOHN'

THREE MONTHS LONG
Mary stayed with
her cousin, then
headed home. -

The day came
and Elzbieta
gave birth to
her son then
her kith and kin,
hearing quite how
the LORD GOD had
shown **her** such mercy
- *they joined her in joy.*

When the eighth day
arrived, it was time for
the boy to be cleansed —

he was just then about to
be called 'Zechariah'
    *like father,*
      **the same.**

However, on hearing
these words, Elizabeth
said: "*That **cannot** be so -
for his name must be '**John**'.* "

"*What do you mean?*"
they responded:

"***Not one of your
blood*** EVER
***bore that name!***"

— Those assembled
made signs to the father
to know what he wanted
to name his own son.

He motioned to them
for a writing tablet, then
shocked them all writing
'**Let 'JOHN' be his name**'.

*Immediately,* IN
THAT SELF-SAME INSTANT —
Zechariah's mouth was opened,
his tongue could speak again
AND **GOD** HE PRAISED.

His neighbors, each
one overwhelmed
with awe - over
all of the hills
of Judea
spread word of
what happened there.

— Every person
who heard about
John exclaimed:

*"What FATE
can **such** a
child have?"*

FOR THE HAND
OF THE LORD
WAS UPON
HIS LIFE.

(L 1:56-66)

## 10. THE SONG OF ZECHARIAH

INSTILLED WITH
the Holy Spirit,
Zechariah spake
in prophecies:

"*God of Israel,* **praise**
*be to Thee,*
*O LORD —*
*for He hath*
*come down*
*to His people,*
*He hath offered*
*them* REDEMPTION.

*Our LORD holds*
*a Savior's bugle*
*aloft in the land*
*of HIS servants -*
*in David's House*

*— as foretold*
  *by His prophets,*
*before it took place.*

*We **have** been delivered
from our foes - **and**
from the blades of
those who hate us.*

*We **must** extend
the* MERCY *that was
promised to our forebears
and **honor** the* PLEDGE *that
had been sworn to our
father -* ABRAHAM:

*that we, being
rescued from our
enemies' clutches, will
do our Lord's bidding,*
AND FREE OF ALL FEAR —

**in sanctity and purity
live before Him
each day of our lives!**

O THOU, *dearest son,
shalt be called
the '*PROPHET
OF GOD ON HIGH*';*

*thou wilt go into*
*the presence*
*of the Lord —*
*prepare the path*
　*= for H*ɪᴍ *=*

*Thou wilt make*
*His people know*
ʀᴇᴅᴇᴍᴘᴛɪᴏɴ - **how**
**all can be freed**
**from their sins.**

*— Only through*
*the tender mercies*
*of our God, through*
*whom the dawning*
*Sun rises to waken us,*
*wilt Thou illumine those*
*who dwell in the darkness*
*and in the shadow of death.*

**Thou guidest**
**our feet upon the path**
**that leadeth**
　　　**unto PEACE."**


(L 1:67-79)

# I. A NEW LIFE

*Once the basket was open
she gazed on the **infant**.*

*Behold! — it wept, and*
SHE HAD **LOVE** FOR IT*!*

EXODUS 2:6

## 11.  A CENSUS FOR CÆSAR

IN THOSE DAYS
Augustus Cæsar
did publicly order
that stock should be
taken of whom Rome
could tax: a *Census of
the Roman Empire* -
the first as Cirenius
governed in Syria.

Thus did everyone
go to their home town
to sign themselves
up to be taxed. —

And so Joseph,
among them, left
Galilee's Nazareth,
going Judea-bound
- Bethlehem - whence
he descended from
DAVID's *House*.

Thither
he travelled
with Mary, to
register them
for the taxes.

At that point - in
marital union bound -
Joseph's wife now was
approaching the end
of her pregnancy.

(L 2:1-5)

## 12. IN THE TOWN OF DAVID

DURING THE DAYS
they were there
in Bethlehem,
*birth was due.*
When the time
came, a boy unto
Mary was born —
their first-born son.

First he was wrapped
up in swaddling cloths,
then placed down beside
them, in manger of stone;

*for*
*there*
*was no*
*guest-room*
*available here, so*
*they had to make do*
*with the animals'*
*quarters, a stable*
*to keep them*
*safe and*
*sound.*

Out in the fields
close by, shepherds
lived, who were watching
their flocks by the light
of the moon —

at that point there
appeareth an angel
to them, of the Lord's,
*and the light of Divinity*
*shone and illumined*
*the space all around*
**- and they gasped**
**in sheer marvel.**

The angel,
it said,
*reassuringly*
then:

"BE YE ALL

NOT IN FEAR,

*For I bring you*

**GOOD NEWS** that

*will make all your*

*people* UNITE

IN JOY.

*For on this day,
in David's town,
**THE SAVIOUR** has
been born to you -
**Anointed One** and
long-awaited **Lord**.*

*— And let this be
a sign for you – a baby
bound up in its swaddling
cloths within a manger
YOU SHALL FIND."*

And at that very instant,
multitudes of angels
stood around
the one who spoke
- all giving praise to God,

announcing:

*"Glory be unto GOD
in Heaven on High
and on Earth — let
Peace reign upon those
whom HE **justly favors**."*

Once the angels of God
had returned to
the Heavens,
the shepherds
spoke straightway
amongst themselves:

" — *We must
make our way
to Bethlehem —*
**WITNESS** *all that
the Lord God
has told us
about.*"

(L 2:6-15)

## 13. SHEPHERDS PAY HOMAGE

SO THEN
all the shepherds
departed, soon finding
both Mary and Joseph
— with Jesus in
manger.

- The moment
that they laid their
eyes on *this child*,
all of them started
to share
the GOOD NEWS

*— and each one*

*who heard them*

*was stunned by*

*the words that*

*the shepherds*

*were speaking.*

*- the shepherds departed, soon finding both Mary and Joseph — with Jesus in manger*

Meanwhile
Mary delighted
at all that occurred
then - *so special* - she
thought on it deep
in her heart.


And the shepherds
went back to their flocks,
praising God in His Glory
for all they had seen
and heard, —

*which had been*
*just exactly*
*as they*
*were forewarned.*


(L 2:16-20)

## 14. "WHERE IS THE NEW KING?"

AND AFTER WHEN
Jesus was born
in Judea —
in Bethlehem,
while Herod
was King,

a group of Magi
from Eastern lands
arrivèd then in
Jerusalem.

Of Herod
they asked:

*"O where is the
newly born 'KING
    OF THE JEWS'?*

*We have followed
His star* **hence**
*we come here
to worship HIM.—"*

Instantly Herod
had heard what
was said **then**
his head set in
turmoil - *and
all of the City.*

Herod called
chief priests and
teachers of Law - to
stand there before him -
to answer him clear: *"**Where**
then - this Holy 'Messiah' -
is **He to be born**?"*

They replied right away:
*"Bethlehem - in Judea",*
for all of them knew
the Prophet's words:

*"Yet ye, in Bethlehem
- Land of Judah - are
by no means the most
modest in that land, for
thence comes a Monarch
— for Israel, their Shepherd."*

"We have followed His star **hence** we come here to worship HIM"

And after that
Herod convened all
three Magi *clandestinely* -

*precisely* learning from
them when HIS STAR
began to shine.

To David's town
   he sent them,
      saying:

"*— Go there and*

*search ye cautiously*

*- then, once you find*

*him, send word back*

*that I may come*

*to* HONOR HIM."


(Mt 2:1-8)

## 15. **THREE MAGI BRING TRIBUTES**

ON HEARING ALL
that Herod bade,
the wise men went
upon their way, —

following the risen star
until it led where
**HE** was born.

Arriving in that place,
the Magi
all exulted finding
HIM.

Stepping within,
they could see
the new baby
- *behold it* -
together with
Mary, its mother;

they bowed down
at once, to pay
HIM tribute.

Then with
their offerings
each one approached
HIM - with treasures
of *gold* and of
*frankincense,*
*myrhh.*

\* \* \* \* \* \*

*The Magi*
*were shown*
*in a dream that*
*they must not return*
*to King Herod again*

*- they **paid heed** to*
*that warning*
*and made*
*their way back*
*by a different route*

AT ONCE.

(Mt 2:9-12)

## 16. A TIME FOR PURIFICATION

THEN, ON
the eighth day
past he was born,
- the time came to
make the boy pure
in God's eyes,

— he was
christened
as 'JESUS' just
as was foretold
by the angel before
his conception.

- After that,
Mary his mother,
went also through rites
of purification —
imposed by
the laws of Moses.

Joseph and Mary,
with Jesus, then
went to Jerusalem,

*there* to present him to
GOD - as is also laid
down in the Law:

"*For every
first-born male,
unto the* LORD *he shall
be consecrated.*"


They went there
as well to give
presents of
sacrifice,

owing to that
which is writ:

"*Give a couple of
doves or a pair
of young pigeons.*"


(L 2:21-24)

## 17. SIMEON'S BLESSING

IN THAT TIME
Simeon dwelt
in the City
- one so
righteous,
pious, devout;

the HOLY SPIRIT, it
rested on him while
awaiting Israel's
consolation.

To Simeon
the SPIRIT spoke
- *reminding him* **he
would not die till God's
'MESSIAH' HAD REVEALED
HIS *face to him.*

Animated by
this thought,
he went toward
the Temple Court

— ***there*** were
Mary and Joseph
with Jesus, in keeping
with custom, to get
the boy blessed.

Simeon then held
the child in his arms
and with words of praise
he prayed to God, saying:

"*Lord Supreme, as
Thou hast promised,
I, Thy servant, may
now be dismissed —*

***at peace*** *– for presently
mine eyes have witnessed
Thy Salvation, One that
T*HOU *hast made for*
EVERY NATION

*—* A ***light*** *for
the enlightenment
of non-believers **and** for
Glorious Splendor of
Thy People,* ***Israel****."*

Every word that
they were told,
the child's parents
heard in awe. —

And after that did
Simeon his blessing
on the boy bestow,
and blessing TO
THEM ALL and
to his mother
Mary; **then
he said**:

*"Your infant son,
the Fates divine,
shall be the cause
of Rise and Fall in
**our nation** - Israel -
a SIGN against whom
many, they shall fight.*

LET INMOST THOUGHTS
OF MANY HEARTS BE LAID
OUT BARE - *FOR THAT WOULD I
SUFFER A SWORD PIERCE MY SOUL!"*

(L 2:25-35)

## 18. ANNA, THE PROPHETESS

AT THE TEMPLE
dwelled also
a *prophetess*
who was
named Anna;
daughter of Penuel
- Asher's tribe.

Ancient in years
was this soothsayer,
seven years only with
husband, a widow -
now *eighty-four*.

— But not one time
ever did Anna depart
from the temple —
she prayed there,
she worshipped,
she fasted - *all
day and all
night.*

At that instant,
                she came up to
Mary and Joseph;
                she told them how
due to their child,
                she made deepest
praise to the Lord.

And Anna
                spoke openly,
happy to
                talk of this boy
who was
                *'**HE** LONG-AWAITED -*

*THE **PEOPLE**'S **REDEMPTION**'.*

(L 2:36-38)

# 19. A DREAM OF EGYPT

SOON AFTER THE MAGI
had come to worship
Jesus and departed,

an angel of the Lord again
appeared to Joseph
in a dream —

*"Quick, get up
and leave!"*
it told him -
*"Begone with
your child and
his mother - - -
**flee to Egypt** NOW!"*

And after that,
the angel added:

*"I warn you, **not
to move from there**
until the day I tell you,
– BEWARE, for Herod, he
is hell-bent on finding
your son to* KILL HIM*!"*

(Mt 2:13)

## 20. **HEROD'S VENOM**

ON REALIZING
they had fled
*without returning
to him* - Herod was
enraged at how
the Magi **so** had
mocked him.

Out of fury,
Herod ordered
all those boys of
two and under ***to
be slaughtered*** —
*those who resided
near Bethlehem.*

He did this due to
knowing what the three
wise men had taught him

- and **thus**,
that spake by Jeremiah
came to be
fulfilled:

*"In Ramah,*

*I hear voices*

*weeping, wails*

*of* LAMENTATION

*— Rachel crying for*

*her children, shunning*

*every word of comfort,*

*- she shall find no solace*

**for her boys are dead**

**and gone,** NO MORE.*"*


(Mt 2:16-18)

*— Rachel crying for her children, shunning every word of comfort, - she shall find no solace*

## 21. A DREAM IN EGYPT

AFTER THE COUNSEL
the Lord's angel
gave him -
Joseph departed
with mother and child

- Bethlehem leaving
beneath cloak of night,
they set on their path
toward Egypt's land.

And there they resided,
as family — just
until after the life of
King Herod had passed.

Thus, yet again,
were the words that
the Lord spake through
prophets come true:

*"For out of Egypt,*
***I have called***
***my Son."***

After Herod
expired, again
did an angel of God
come to Joseph, to give
him this warning:

*"Go, take your family,*
*wife and son with you,*
RETURN NOW TO ISRAEL —

*those who had sought thy*
*child's life* **have gone**.*"*

(Mt 2:14-15; 19-20)

*Joseph departed
with mother and child
- Bethlehem leaving
beneath cloak of night*

## 22. 'A NAZARENE'

— SO JOSEPH THEN LEFT
and went back with his wife
and their son to Israel.

*However, on hearing*
*that, after*
*his death,*
*Archeläus*
*now reigned*
*in King Herod's place*

- **he froze with fear.**

After the vision he saw
in his dream,
Joseph moved them
to Galilee —

*and there they dwelled*
*and made their home*
*the town of **Nazareth**.*

So thus were fulfilled
the prophet's words:

"He shall be called a **Nazarene**."

- Joseph and Mary
had done all that God
wished and followed
the Law when they
lived out in Egypt.


Nazareth, hometown,
where they would all live
— there the child, he grew,
*both in body and wisdom;*

the **Grace** of **God**

WAS UPON HIM.


(Mt 2:21-23 / L 2:39-40)

## 23. JESUS IS LOST

EVERY YEAR
Jesus' parents would
go to Jerusalem,
celebrate Passover's
feast: the *Pesach*.

In that year
(as their boy
reached twelve)
they went - as was
custom - back there,
      to Jerusalem.

Once rituals
were over then
Mary, with Joseph,
went onwards home —
unaware that their son had
remained in the city,

far  behind  them.

Believing that he
*was still with them,*
they travelled on further,
for one day more —

yet when they asked
around they found out
that their family, friends,
**no-one** had seen Jesus.

Immediately,
they headed back,
in the search of their
*now missing son -*
**to Jerusalem.**


(L 2:41-45)

## 24. "IN MY FATHER'S HOUSE"

IT WAS NOT UNTIL AFTER
three whole days
had passed,
they discovered
their son — he was
standing amid the teachers.

The rabbis and experts
in law were around him -
he followed their words and
asked multiple questions. —

When all those surrounding
him heard what he said,
they were stunned
by the depths of his
wisdom: his KNOWING.

Then, when his parents
caught sight of him,
*they too were*
*truly astounded.*

*they were stunned by the depths of his wisdom: his KNOWING*

Mary, his mother, asked Jesus:

*"O why, dearest son, hast thou*
*caused us such anguish? -*
*your father and I,*
*we have gone*
*through anxiety*
*seeking to find you."*

To which the young
Jesus, untroubled,
        replied:

*"For whyever could*
*you both not find me? —*
**Did you not think** *that I may*
*be in my Father's house?"*

- But they could not
make sense of what Jesus,
their boy, meant to say
through these words
that he told them.

      (L 2:46-50)

## 25. OBEDIENCE AND WISDOM

BY THE TIME
Jesus travelled
beside his parents
upon the path
to Nazareth,

all he had done
was in keeping with
discipline - each day
obeying what he
had been asked.

Nonetheless, all
that his mother
had witnessed him do,
— *in her heart*
*it was cherished.*

From a boy
Jesus grew and
he rose in his stature,

— in height and
in wisdom he found
he was favored by
men and by God.

Yet it was not
until he had reached
thirty years
that the man, Jesus -
grown and
matured - started out
on his path,
*his own ministry leading.*

(L 2:51-52; 3:23)

## II. 'THE ANOINTED ONE'

*Touch Not*
*My Anointed Ones*
*— unto my Prophets*
DO NO HARM

PSALMS 105:15

## 26. THE WORD OF GOD

THE SON OF
Zechariah grew —
in spirit strong became.

*In the reign of Tiberius -*
*Year 15 - while Judea*
*was governed by*
*Pontius Pilate,*

*while Herod the Tetrarch*
*in Galilee reigned and*
*his brother,*
*King Philip,*
*Iturea and Traconitis*
*ruled - Lysanias,*
*monarch of*
*Abilene,*

*during*
*the priesthood*
*of Annas and*
*Caiaphas.* —

***Then***
*was when*
*John heard*
*God's Word in*
*in the wilderness;*

waiting to preach
to the people
of Israel

- he lived
in the desert
until it was time.

Then
he appeared
on the banks of
the Jordan:

teaching,
baptizing —
redeeming from sins.


(L 1:80; 3:1-3)

## 27. "MAKE READY THE WAY"

A DAY
of Good News
has now dawned
upon us

of Jesus
- *the Christ* -
the Anointed One;

for the SON OF GOD,
as foretold by Isaiah:

'I send Thee a herald
to light Thy road.

*Dost Thou hear
the voice of one
who calls out from
the desolate plains? -*

"**Make ready the way
of the LORD, - for
His paths you must
make straight!**" '

*"Repent! The Kingdom
of Heaven is nigh! —"*

announces the voice of
this man from the wild

Thus did the Baptist emerge
from the wilderness:
JOHN, who would preach
the forgiveness of sins.

In the waters he purged
the hearts of sinners,
christening all in
repentance come.

        All     of
        Judea
        and
all of Jerusalem

came out to find him,

professing their sins -

in the river of Jordan

their souls were

redeemed

*through*

*the power*

*of God's absolution.*

*"Repent! The Kingdom
of Heaven is nigh! —"*

announces the voice of
this man from the wild:

*"Each valley is filled,
each mount abased,
the crooked is straight
and rough now smooth*

*— all of you people
I bring the **news** —
God's Advent of
SALVATION!"*

In raiments knit
from hair of camel
- a band of leather
around his waist -

surviving on locusts
and honeys of nature,
John, on the Jordan,
baptized *every day.*

To Bethabara they
came in their hordes,
holy leaders come also
to meet with John —

Pharisees,
Sadducees,
Levites and more,
from Jerusalem, all
had this question
for him:
>"*WHO ART THOU?*"

Straight away did John,
of his own will, confess:

"*— I'm not the 'Messiah',
I am not* **The One**."

"*Then are you Elijah?
or Are you the Prophet?*"

To each of these queries
did John respond, "*No*".

In total frustration they
asked him: "*Then WHO?
We must bring back
an answer to those
who have sent us!*

- ***Who do you say
that you*** REALLY ARE*?*"

Instead of
his own words,
John quoted Isaiah:

*"Mine is
whose voice cries
aloud from the wilderness:*

**'Make straight
the path for the Lord!'"**

    \*       \*       \*       \*

Now some Pharisees
who had been sent
there expressly,
re-questioned
him now in
a different way:

*"If you're no 'Messiah'*
**- then
why the anointing?**

*If you're no Elijah,*
**then why
do you
speak like
the Prophet thus?"**

Stepping forth toward
crowds who
awaited
anointing,
John spake to
the Pharisees,
Sadducees - *words
with flames ablazing*:

**"Ye nest of vipers!**
*- who warned ye to
flee from the wrath
yet to come?! —*

*Produce the fruit
of repentance,*
**not sentences
hollow and numb!**

*— Do not start off
by telling yourselves,
so entitled:* 'ABRAHAM,
HE IS OUR FATHER ALONE

- WE CAN DO NO WRONG - '

*For I tell ye that
out of these stones themselves
God can fashion
new children for him!"*

*For the blade of the axe
is struck hard
at the roots*

*- every tree
that produces
bad fruit is hacked
down and consigned to*
                             *the*
                                   *FLAMES!"*

    \*        \*        \*        \*

*"Then what should we do?"*

asked the masses
there gathered,

and John spoke
to all of the people thus:

*"Whoever hath two shirts*
*- **give one who has none***

      *and*

*whoever hath food, **share***
***with those - without!"***

Collectors of taxes
came there too for
baptism, quizzing John:

"*What must we also do?*"

- He replied: "*Do not
take one bit more than
you're meant to —
tax only the money
that's truly due!*"

Even soldiers were
stood there
and also
called out
to him: "*John,
tell us, what must we do?*"

To whom he responded:

" *- Do not coerce money
when that is extortion.*

*Do not bear false witness
where none are to blame*

*— and Finally,* **be thou
content with your pay!**"

People on all hands
were waiting
expectantly,

many were
wondering:

*"Is He the C*HRIST*?"*


John could
sense all of their
questioning hearts,
so he stood up and
answered the
populace
thus:


*"I am the one who baptizes
with W*ATER*, that all
may repent of
their sins*

*but after
comes One far
more mighty than I
Who baptizes with F*IRE

*and the* H*OLY* S*PIRIT*

*— In your midst steps
the One in whose presence
I dwindle, the straps of whose
shoes I'm not fit to undo -*

*nay, whose sandals
I'm not even
worthy to
hold!*

*See, in His hand
is a harvesting fork,
to separate out all
the grain from
the chaff -*

*with this
does He clear
the threshing floor -*

*storing wheat in His barns*

*as unstoppable fires
burn husks
to ash - "*

With these
and with other words
John unveiled all the GOOD NEWS
he had learned to his brethren there —

(M 1:1-8 / Mt 3:1-12 / L 3:4-18 / J 1:19-28)

## 28. 'THE LAMB OF GOD'

AND AT
THAT TIME
Jesus of Nazareth
came up the banks of
the Jordan - from Galilee.

When
John saw
Him walking
towards him, he
uttered these words:

*"Behold -*

*the Lamb of God,*
*He who cleanses ALL SIN*
*from the World —*

*Here is the One*
*Whom I meant*
*when I said:*

**'The One who**
**comes after me**
**comes above me**
**because He came**
**before me.' — "**

But when
Jesus arrived
before John
in person,

the Baptist
immediately
said to Him
this:

*"It is I
and not You
who have
need of
anointing
- yet YOU
come to
me?"*

*"Yes I do,"*

answered Jesus:

**"that's how it must be**

**for only in this way will
each act of God's plan
be reached with
perfection".**

John no longer
deterred Him and
promptly complied.

- Thus
was Jesus
baptized
by John in
the Jordan - who
afterward spoke of
what happened like this:

*"At the moment
He rose from
the waters,
the heavens above
opened             wide.*

*What I saw
was
the
SPIRIT
of
GOD
coming
down
in
the
form
of*

a dove

**- on His forehead
it rests.**

*At the moment He rose from the waters, the heavens above opened wide*

*He
looked
to the skies
in prayer as it
sat there — a voice
from above spake forth:*

*'I AM WELL PLEASED
WITH YOU -
**MY SON***

*- WITH YOU
WHOM I LOVE '."*

Then
John, he
reflected:

*"Before we had met
**here** I never had known*

Hᴉᴍ.

*For **what reason** had I
'The Baptist' become*

*— than **anoint**
the 'ᴍᴇssɪᴀʜ'
for our Holy
Land? -"*

After, John
spoke to many
of what he had seen:

*"I myself did not know Him
but HE who first sent me
to baptize with water,
HE told me before -*

*'When you
WITNESS
the SPIRIT
d e s c e n d
upon Him
- KNOW HE
IS THE ONE
who baptizes
with SPIRIT"*

- I SAW WITH
MY EYES
AND I TESTIFY
HERE -

THAT THIS WAS
IN TRUTH
GOD's
UNIQUE
CHOSEN ONE."

(M 1:9-11 / Mt 3:13-17 / L 3:21-22 / J 1:29-34)

## 29. FOLLOWERS OF JESUS

THE SUCCEEDING MORN
again
John was there and
he
pointed out Jesus
to
two of his followers:

*"There, don't you see,
He who passes —
the Lamb of God?"*

On hearing this,
both of them
went after Jesus
and followed behind;

noticing them,
He turned round
and He asked them:

*"What do you want?"*
and they bowed,
saying: *"Rabbi…*

*O teacher, just tell us
please, where are
you staying?"*

*"Come hither,
I'll show you"*,
to them He replied

- so they went
right along and saw
where He was lodged,

and they spent
the whole day with
Him, till it was dusk.

Andrew - the brother
of Simon - was
one of the two who
had heard what John said;

after following Jesus,
he sought out his brother
to tell him: *"Dear Simon,
the CHRIST has been found!"*

And once he had found him,
he brought him to Jesus,
who looked in his eyes and
said:
    *"Simon,* **hear me**
*- son of John - I'll call
you now* **'Cephas'**,
*Peter, the Rock."*

Jesus,
the next day,
He made a decision
to make His way to Galilee.

Leaving,
He met up with
Philip and said to him:

"Come now and follow me."

Like Peter and Andrew,
he came from
Bethsaida,

on finding Nathanael,
he shared what
he knew:

*"At last*
 *we have found*
 *He whom Moses*
 *has written of, —*
 *One of whom also*
 *the Prophets spake:*
 *Jesus of Nazareth -*
 *Joseph's son."*

*"From Nazareth!*
**What good e'er hailed
from there?!"**

On hearing
his harsh exclamation
did Jesus
step close to Nathanael,
saying:

*"In truth, stands
an Israelite
here
in whom
lies no deceit. —"*

*"But how do
you know me?"*
said he, turned to Jesus:

*"There I observed you,
sitting 'neath
the fig tree's shade,
then Philip called you."*

Nathanael spoke aloud,
proclaiming:
        *"*K<small>ING OF</small> I<small>SRAEL</small>
<small>ART</small> T<small>HOU</small>, R<small>ABBI</small> - **S<small>ON OF</small> G<small>OD</small>!***"*

To which
Jesus answered:

*"Though you believe*
*since I told you of*
**how I knew you**
**before we met** -

TRULY SHALT THOU
WITNESS THINGS
FAR GREATER —
MORE AWESOME
THAN WORDS CAN SAY."

Then He concluded:

*"Verily, I say to thee:*

*thine eyes will behold*

*the Heavens open -*

*Angels of God*

*ascend and*

*descend -*

*the* SON OF MAN

**thine eyes shall see!"**

(J 1:35-51)

## 30. A WEDDING MIRACLE

THREE DAYS AFTER
Jesus had been baptized,
there occurred then at Cana
- in Galilee - a wedding party,
a *GRAND CELEBRATION*, that
Mary was attending.

— Jesus came too
with his followers, for
they were also invited
to join this feast. —

However, once wine had
run dry, Mary turned
to her son, saying:

*"Son, don't you see,
they have run
out of wine!"*

*"Mother - WHY
dost thou ask that
of me **at this moment**? -*

***The time I***
***should do this***
*IS NOT YET UPON ME."*

In spite of that,
Mary, she turned
to the servants
and asked: *"Do*
*whatever he tells*
*you to do. —* "

Not far from them
stood several
waters jars,
six or so
made of
the stone
that is used
during *cleansing*
as part of Judaic rites.

Each held upwards from
*eighty full litres,*
one jar - **over thirty gallons.**

Jesus then turned
to the servers
in bidding them:

*"Fill every jar to*
*the top with water."*

Filled were they all until
water flowed over the brims
- at which point Jesus
said, in instructing
them thus:

*"Fill one vessel*
*and take it right over to*
**he who is leading the banquet."**

This was done and
the Master — partaking
of what he was passed —
*saw that there was still wine.*

He was puzzled for *he had*
*believed* **only**
**water** *remained by then.*

"— Yet you — *you have saved up the finest of wines* TO THE END OF THE FEAST!"

*Yet the servants themselves*
**knew** *where this wine*
*had come from*
- THE WATERS
THEY HAD JUST DRAWN OFF.

At that point did
the head of the feast
take the groom to one side
and exclaim to him:

" *- How like custom it is*
*that the very best wine*
*is brought out at the start*
*and the worse only later,*
*once guests are so tipsy*
THAT THEY CAN'T TELL.

*— Yet you —* ***you have***
***saved up the finest of wines***
TO THE END OF THE FEAST*!"*

(J 2:1-12)

A UNIFIED GOSPEL IN ENGLISH VERSE

# III. A NEW MESSAGE

*The Lord thy God
shall bring forth a Prophet
who is **of your people***

- HEED HIS WORD

DEUTERONOMY 18:15

## 31. **TEMPTATIONS OF SATAN**

JESUS, IMBUED WITH
the *Holy Spirit*, now left
the banks of the Jordan behind.

The *Spirit* forced Jesus
out
into the wilds —
for
forty days and
for
forty nights. -

In the desert
he dwelled
and he ate
and drank
nothing -
for *every*
*one* of
those
forty
days

*there*
he lived with
the creatures of nature
and lay down his body to
rest alongside them.

Throughout
all that time did
the devil tempt him
- while angels watched
over with utmost concern.

Forthwith,
post forty days,
Jesus was famished
- the *mighty deceiver*
would test him
once more:

"*If - in all truth -
you are
God's OWN SON,
then
turn this stone
to
a loaf of bread!*"

To which
Jesus replied:

"*Remember, before,
it was clearly written -*

'MAN SURVIVES NOT UPON
BREAD ALONE — BUT ON
EACH WORD THAT COMES
FROM THE MOUTH OF GOD'"

"— *If thou art truly the Son of* GOD, *then throw yourself down on the Holy City*"

So the tempter
led Jesus up high
on a mountainside,
showing to him
all the world and
its kingdoms:

"*You I shall give*
*all the power*
*and glory!*
*I have been*
*given this —*
**it can be yours!**
*All you need do*
*is to bow down*
*and worship* ME
*-* EVERYTHING *then*
**shall belong to you!**"

to which Jesus retorted:

"*Fall behind me Satan!*
*In scriptures it says —*
'THOU MUST WORSHIP
THE LORD THY GOD
- AND THOU MUST
SERVE ONLY HIM',"

Then finally
Jesus was led
to Jerusalem —
there, at the peak
of the Temple was
placed by the devil who
taunted him once again:

"— *If thou art truly*
*the Son of GOD, then*
*throw yourself down*
*on the Holy City -*
*for it has been*
　　*written:*

'THE LORD SHALL
COMMAND THAT
THE ANGELS
AROUND YOU
DO WATCH YOU
ATTENTIVELY —
HOLD YOU ALOFT IN
THEIR HANDS - THAT
YOUR FEET WILL NOT
STRIKE ANY STONES'."

- At last,
one more time,
Jesus answered
to Satan:

"*It also says -*

'TEST
NOT
THY
LORD
ON
HIGH'"

— At this point
the tempter was
done with his
tempting,
he left,
*though*
*he would*
*return* **when**
**the time came.**

Now
the angels drew near
to Jesus,
and tended to him.

(M 1:12-13 / Mt 4:1-11 / L 4:1-13)

# 32. "DESTROY THIS TEMPLE, I WILL RAISE IT UP!"

AS TIME NEARED TO
honor the Passover,
Jesus made way
to Jerusalem;

but there, within
the Temple Court,
he found in its place
*a market fair!* —

The wares on
display were so
many and various:
sheep and
    doves and
        cattle,
*so many things more;*

the changers of money
were also set up in
the buying and selling
of currencies there.

Entwining cords together,
Jesus made
a makeshift whip and
chased
the traders out the Temple Court.

    Out were driven
        cattle,
            sheep
                and men,
    the tables overturned
    — the coins of all
    the money-changers
    scattered everywhere.

    At those who charged
    for their doves
    he yelled:
        *"Flee*
      *with your birds*
    *from my Father's house*
    *and stop turning it into*
      *a common bazaar!"*

*Entwining cords together,
Jesus made
a makeshift whip and
chased
the traders out the Temple Court*

Of this time
his disciples recalled,
it was written:

*"Fervor for* **THY HOUSE**
**shall devour me.***"*

The Jews, in response
to his actions,
demanded then:

*"Show us some signs of*
*your right* ***to act thus!****"*

To which Jesus responded
with only these words:

*"Destroy this Temple -*
*I* WILL RAISE IT UP AGAIN
IN JUST THREE DAYS.*"*

*"What are you talking*
*about?"* they replied:

*"It took forty-six*
*years to create*
*this place —*

*so **who** can rebuild it
in just three days?"*

But the Temple
he spoke of -
it was his body.

*Only once
Jesus rose up
from the dead* did
disciples remember
the words he had
said to them
**way back
then.**

All of
this made
them believe in
    *the **truth** of
the* SCRIPTURES
— in words
that Jesus
spoke.

It was during this *Pesach*
- as Jesus remained here -
that *many saw miracles*
*which he performed*
**— *and began to***
***believe in his name*.**

However, at that
point in time he
would not give
his trust to them,
inwardly knowing
the way of mankind.

*He did not require*
  *a human witness*
    *for* ***Jesus knew***
      *what dwelt*
        *in each*
          *person's heart.*


(J 2:13-25)

## 33. 'TO BE BORN ANEW'

— IN THAT TIME
there was a Pharisee
whose name was
*Nicodemus*,
a member of
the Holy Council
- one night came
to Jesus, saying:

*"All of us, O Rabbi,
know that Thou art
one whose teachings
come from God Above!*

— WHO ELSE COULD DO
*such miracles as you enact,*
**were not the Holy LORD**
*indwelling every act?"*

To which
Jesus answered:

*"Verily, I say to thee,
that none may view
God's kingdom **lest
they're born anew."***

***"But how can one
be 'BORN ANEW'
whose life is aged?"***

asked Nicodemus:

*"Entering the mother's
womb again, from
whence they came:
SUCH CANNOT BE!"*

And Jesus said, to
make things clear:

*"Forsooth, I tell thee,
none may enter in
God's Kingdom who
is not **reborn** - ANEW -
of SPIRIT **and of Water**;
flesh creates flesh and
the SPIRIT births SPIRIT!*

*Confuse not
my words: 'Thou
must be born again'.*

*The wind will blow
where it will -
none can say
whence it cometh
or whither it goeth —*
**so true of the Spirit too**.*"*

*"But how is that?"*
replied then
Nicodemus:

*"***In all truth***
I say to thee,
thereof we speak
although we know
whereof we have seen
- we testify yet still
thy people won't
accept a word
we say.*

*Of matters earthly*
*I have spoken*
*to thee **yet***
***thou still***
***dost not believe**!*
*How far less possible*
*to speak to thee*
*of things*
*beyond!*

*Not one*
*soul more has*
*gone to Heaven,*
*save the one who first*
*came from there – of*
*whom I speak?*

    *- the '*S<small>ON OF</small> M<small>AN</small>*'.*

*And just as Moses*
*raised a serpent in*
*the wilds, the same*
*way shall the 'Son of*
*Man' be raised on high -*

*that all who have belief
in Him may have
Eternal Life
thereby.*

*For God
has made a gift
unto this world of
His unique and only Son
- because he loves
the World -
in order that
whosoever shall
believe in Him will
perish not* **but live
the** LIFE ETERNAL.

*NOT to damn this world
did Yahweh send
His son here —
but by that means
to save it. Whichever
one believes in Yahweh*
SHALL **NOT BE CONDEMNED**

*- Yet whosoever puts
no faith in Yahweh's
sole begotten Son **is
damned already**.*

*The verdict
has been read:*

LIGHT HAS ENTERED
THE WORLD YET TOO MANY
ADORED THE DARKNESS
IN ITS PLACE BECAUSE
THEIR DEEDS WERE
DARK AND EVIL.

*Whoever does* EVIL
*despises the* LIGHT *and
avoids its glare for **fear**
their deeds will be exposed -*

*But those who live their lives
through* TRUTH *shall enter
in the* LIGHT, *that all may
see what they have done
within the* EYES *of* GOD."

(J 3:1-21)

## 34. **JESUS BAPTIZING**

AFTER JESUS
had spoken with Nicodemus,
then He and followers
went to the plains, far afield,
in Judea's lands —

there he remained with them,
there he baptized - while
the Baptist continued
at Aenon, anointing
the folk of Salim.

In that place flowed
abundantly waters and
*many were coming
to be baptized.*

All this preceded the time
that the baptist was
thrown into prison -
when conflict broke out
between various factions.

For John's followers did not
agree with the ways
of a certain Jew\*
in the matter
of cleansing
— *how rites **should** be done.*

As a unified group they came up
to see John for
they sought
a response to their query,
so one of them spoke up thus:

*"O Teacher, the one who*
*stood with you on*
*Jordan's far side,*
*yes, the one*
*whom you*
*spoke of*
*before he*
*appeared,*
*see there,*
***he baptizes***
*all those who go to him*
*— what do you think of this?"*

\* Meaning 'Jesus'

And to this John
the Baptist replied:

"*Every human receives
only THAT WHICH IS GIVEN
to them - by HEAVEN above.*

*Do you all not recall
that my prophecies
said : 'I am not
The Messiah,
but walk right
in front of the path
he shall tread' ?*

*For truly,
the Bride - she
belongs to the Groom -
while the guests
who attend
His Party
await — listen
out for Him – JOYOUS
are they when they*
**hear His Voice.**

*And in just the same way*
*is such joy **also mine***
*— yes, **my joy is***
COMPLETE. —

*While He has*
*to grow **greater** –*
*I must become **lesser**.*

*The One from Above,*
HE COMES ABOVE
EVERYONE.

*Born of the Earth,*
*thus He speaks like*
*all humans, - yet*
*He from Above,*
*He shall be*
*Above All.*
***He bears***
***witness to***
***what he has***
***seen and heard** —*
YET STILL NO-ONE ACCEPTS
                    HIS WORDS.

— *Whosoever
embraces the words
He says* **confirms Truth
in its highest form,**
*in the fullness
of GOD.* —

*He whom God has sent
down here - He speaks
with God's words,
for God gives Him
His Spirit,* **so boundless.**

*As a Father,
adoring His Son,
He puts everything
into His hands.* —

*Who believes in the Son,
gains* **Life Eternal** —
*who spurns Him are
blind to* **Real Life** *and
shall suffer the wrath of GOD
— it shall rain down upon them."*

(J 3:22-36)

## 35. THE WELL OF LIFE ETERNAL

JESUS KNEW THEN
that the Pharisees
heard he was baptizing
*more than John*;

his disciples increased
in their number, and
they were the ones
who were carrying
out the anointments.

Jesus required to
go through Samaria,
leaving Judea, returning
to Galilee once again. —

He arrived at the town
known as Sychar,
not far from
the plot
Jacob gifted
to Joseph, *his son*.

*There* 'Jacob's Well',
it survived to that day,
and so Jesus sat down
by it, weary for rest
from the journey
just travelled -

by then, it was
nearing on noon.

— A Samaritan woman
came up to draw water
and Jesus requested
of her: "*Wilt thou
     please give
     some water to
     quench my thirst?*"

His disciples right then
had gone off to the town
to bring back some supplies.

Yet the woman
responded to Jesus:
"*But you are a **Jew** and
myself a Samaritan woman!*

*"I tell you, all those who come here to partake of this well — they will surely be thirsty again"*

*How can you ask me
to give you a drink?"*

(for the Jews never mix
with Samaritans. **Never**.)

To this, Jesus
answered: "*If thou
wert aware of the gift
God has given you and
of **who asks you** to do
Him this favor —*

*then you yourself
would ask Him
**just the same**,
and He would
provide you with
l i v i n g   w a t e r .*"

To that the Samaritan
woman replied: "*Yet thou
hast not a vessel with which
to draw water — and truly
this well is profoundly deep.*

*Whence wilt thou draw  
this 'Living Water' of  
which you speak? -*

*Are **You** the One  
GREATER THAN  
JACOB, OUR FATHER,  
who made us this well  
and who drank from it also*

*- as all of his sons did,  
his animals too?"*

*— And then  
Jesus responded:*

*"I tell you, all those  
who come here to  
partake of this well —  
they will surely be thirsty  
again — yet **those ones**  
who drink of the water  
    I give,*

    **THEY SHALL**

    **NEVER THIRST AGAIN.**

*Truly, the water
I bring you,
its* SOURCE
*in your soul
shall expand
into* LIFE ETERNAL.*"*

The Samaritan
now said to Jesus:

*"Dear Sir, I beseech thee
please give me such water so
then I might never be
thirsty again —*
**and then
no more times
need I to visit this well.***"*

Jesus said to her:

*"Go now and bring
back thy husband."*

*"But I have no husband"*,
she answered
at once.

"*I know that,*"
  said Jesus.

"*It's true that
  you have not
  a husband, —
  yet you have had
  five men before and
  the one whom you live
  with, **nor is he** your husband*

  *- so what you have told me
  is thoroughly true.*"

"*Master, I see Thou art
  truly a Prophet*",
  and then
  she went on,
  in replying to him:

"*Our ascendants did worship
  atop of this mountain,
  yet ye who are Jews
  claim the spot
  we must worship
  is **there** in Jerusalem.*"

Jesus then answered
to all she had said:

"*Dear woman,
have faith
in the words
I have told you;
the time is approaching
when thou shalt give praise
to GOD - your Father -
not **here** on this
mountain nor
**there** - in Jerusalem.*

*Ye, the Samaritans, pray
to what you **do not know***

*while we Jews worship
**that which we know.***

*— Understand, that
SALVATION, it cometh
**from the Jews** - yet I tell
thee, the time, it approacheth
(upon us already in truth) when
true worshippers, **they shall give praise
to the Father** — in SPIRIT and TRUTH.*

– These are the
**ideal worshippers**
that the Father seeketh.

GOD is the SPIRIT
– to praise Him, one
has to revere Him in
SPIRIT and TRUTH."

To Jesus,
the woman
then finally said:

"I know the Messiah
is on His way, and
I know that when
He arrives —
THEN everything
will be explained to us."

At which Jesus declared
to her: "I, WHO SPEAK
WITH YOU NOW —
I AM THAT ONE."

(J 4:1-26)

## 36. THE HARVEST OF ETERNAL LIFE

AT THAT MOMENT,
his followers
came back to Jesus —
so stunned
on returning to find him
conversing
with **her** - a Samaritan -
yet not
a single one asked of him:

*"What are you doing?"*

      or

*"Why do you speak
with this woman
— no Jew?"*

And then,
she did not even
pick up her water jar
- walking straight back
to her town, speaking
out to the people
upon her return:

*"Come with me now*
*to meet one who*
*knows **all that***
***I have ever done***
*— it might be that*
*He is the Anointed One!"*

So the people departed
their homes to
make way to
where Jesus still was.

All the while,
disciples of his
tried persuading
him:
   *"Rabbi, you need*
*to have something to eat."*

Yet to them he responded
thus: *"Food do I have*
*that can nourish,*
*of which*
*you know nothing yet."*

- Jesus's followers
looked at each other
confused, saying: "*Has
someone **already** made
him some food? —* "

But immediately
Jesus explained to them:
"*My 'food' means doing
the bidding of* H<small>E</small>
*who has sent me*
**- to finish what
needs to be done**.

*Don't you know
the familiar proverb:*

'*— For months still
remain before time
comes for harvest*'?

**So listen** *and unclose
your eyes and gaze out
on the fields — how ready
are they for the harvest!*

*Even at this time,
the ones who reap
crops make a living
— for Life Eternal –
so reaper and sower
may both be pleased*
**with what they do.**

*- Therefore,
the saying that
'While the one sows
does another one reap'*
**is completely true.**

*I am making you
go out to harvest
what you have*
**not yet sown -**

*others have done
the hard work and
you reap the results
of their labors now."*


(J 4:27-38)

## 37. NEW BELIEVERS

DUE TO WHAT
the Samaritan woman
had told them,
the townsfolk *began*
***to believe***
    *in Jesus*:

*"He told me
each thing I have
**ever done** — every act
of my past **he knew**!"*

Therefore, many
Samaritans
came up to Jesus
and tried to convince
him *to stay with them* —

and he stayed two more days
for the depth of
his knowing convinced
many there
*to believe in him.*

The people did not
tell the woman:

"*We give him our faith
　due to all that
　you told us.*"

**No,**
　they said:

"*We give him faith
　due to what
　we have
　heard
　**for ourselves.***

*We know that
this man,* **in all truth,**
*brings* SALVATION -
*that he is the* SAVIOR *of
Our World.*"


(J 4:39-42)

## 38. THE BAPTIST IMPRISONED

AFTER
Jesus heard
John had been
thrown into prison,
he went back to Galilee,
preaching the *Good
News* that came
from God.

Herod
the Tetrarch
arrested the Baptist —
then shackled and bound
him, threw into a cell —
all as *Herodias*, wife
of King Philip,
the brother
of Herod,
complained
and objected to
what John was saying
*to Herod himself* - that:

*"Your marriage with her*
*— it breaks the Law."*

Herod
had wanted
**to have him killed**
yet in fear of the people
declined to act, for so many
believed that the Baptist
was *truly* **no less**
than a Holy
Prophet.

After John
censured him
*for his union* and
for sins of other kinds
— Herod decided to do
one more thing that
would add to
these ills,

*by **jailing** the Baptist.*

(M 1:14 / Mt 4:12; 14:3-5/ L 3:19-20 / J 3:24)

"*upon those who were hid in the shadows of Death — NEW LIGHT has shone - a **New Day** has dawned -* "

# 39. "REPENT, THE KINGDOM OF GOD IS NIGH"

AND FROM
that day forth
Jesus started to say:

*"Repent, for*
*the Kingdom of God*
*is nigh - confess*
*all your Sins and believe*
*in the Good News*
*— FOR IT IS **TRUE**!"*

Nazareth leaving now
far behind him,
Jesus moved
onwards -
**Capernaum**
would be where
he lived - by the lake
near Naphtali and Zebulum
— such
that the words
of Isaiah, the seer,
*they would **thus** be fulfilled:*

"In the land of Naphtali,
the land of Zebulum,
over the Jordan —
beyond the Path
of the Lake:
the **Galilee
of Gentiles** –
those who lived,
lost in the darkness,
behold now GREAT LIGHT;

upon those who were
hid in the shadows of Death
   — NEW LIGHT has shone,
    a **New Day** has dawned."

(M 1:15 / Mt 4:13-17)

## 40. "THY SON SHALL LIVE!"

ONCE TWO DAYS
had passed, Jesus
parted for Galilee.

He himself knew, and
explained to others, that
*there are no prophets with
fame, **in their own town**.*

However, as soon as
he set foot among
his own people,
they welcomed
him back, *made
him feel at home.*

They had seen
his accomplishments
out in Jerusalem -
during the Passover, when
they were there.

Now he had
come back to
Cana in Galilee —
there, where he transmuted
*water* to *wine.*

- In that town there
then lived a Roman official,
one Royal, whose son, in
Capernaum, lay gravely ill.

The instant
word reached him
that Jesus
had come from Judea
and that
he was dwelling in
Galilee -
***he*** *sought him out,*
and
implored him to come
and to heal
his son who lay
close to the tomb.

Jesus said: "*Is it true
that your people
shall never believe it
when miracles
happen - in front of
your eyes are
enacted -* **not even then?**"

The Royal official
still pressed him though,
asking: "*Come with me sir,
please come and help me
lest my son should die!*"

At which Jesus said:

"**Go now!
Thy son shall live!**"

So the man asked
no more of him -
putting full faith
in his words -
and he left.

During the journey
returning home,
he was met by
his servants
who brought
him *good news*:

**his son was alive.**

On inquiring exactly
the time when
his son had
recovered,
a servant
responded:

*"The day prior,*
*almost an hour*
*gone noon -* **then**
*the fever, it left him."*

    — It was now that
the father would realize
***that*** *was the moment*
*when Jesus had said:*
  **"Thy son shall live!"**

So, because of all this,
*those who lived **in***
***this household**,*
put all of their
*FAITH* in
Jesus.

This was
the *second*
of various signs
that he worked after
parting Judea
and living
in Galilee.


(J 4:43-54)

## 41. A RABBI MOST UNWELCOME

WHEN JESUS HAD FINISHED
recounting these stories,
he parted that place
and went onwards, home.

- Some followers then
did accompany him
back to Nazareth,
where he had
grown — from
a child to youth and
from youth into man.

The word of the *Spirit*
had brought him
to Galilee —
news of
his coming
spread far and wide:

*all heard Jesus was*
**on his way**
**back here** NOW.

Arriving there,
Sabbath approached
so he went up to
preach in the synagogue,
as was his wont

— the populace
were simply lost for words
and all praised him
his wisdom beyond compare:

"*What a true gift of* KNOWING
*this young man possesses*
*- whence comes this and*
*all his miraculous powers?*"

People said to each other:

"*Is this one, who works*
*such great wonders*
*not son of the carpenter*
*— Joseph's boy?*"

"*Yes, that's right, for*
*his mother is Mary and*

*he is the brother to Joseph,*
*James, Simon and*
*Judas - don't*
*all of his sisters*
*live with us here too?"*

*"Wherefrom then*
*did this Jesus*
*obtain his talents?"*

Taking his place to read,
a scroll of Isaiah
- the prophet -
was passed to him.

— On unrolling it
Jesus then read out the passage
wherein it is writ: "*The Spirit*
*of the Lord is upon me -*
*for he has anointed me so*
*as to preach the* GOOD NEWS
*to the poor. I am sent to proclaim*
*liberation to those imprisoned,*
*regaining of sight*
              *by the blind*

*and the freedom*
  *of those oppressed —*

*I make my pronouncement*
  *for* **this year**,
    *consecrated by*
      *the* L*ORD* *Above.*"

After reading,
he rolled up the scroll,
passed it back to the beadle
and then sat down.

As all eyes in the temple
were fixed upon him -
Jesus started saying:

"On **this day**
  that scripture is
  brought to fulfillment
  while each of you listens
    to what I say."

Not an ill word was said
about Jesus —

for all were so awestruck
   as eloquence
      flowed from his lips,
   yet still some said:

"*Surely, this Jesus is Joseph's son?*"

— Upon taking stock
of this,
many became quite upset -
Jesus,
seeing this, spoke up and said
to them:
      *"Truly a prophet will*
      *never lack honor*
      *except in his*
      *own town —*
      ***'mid relatives* and**
      **within his own home.**"

At the realization
   of just who he was
      as he spoke to them
   thus, *they were hateful*
— resented him now.

Jesus then said to them:
"*Certainly you shall*
*prescribe me*
*the maxim:*
*'**Physician,***
***Heal Thyself!**'*
*and you also shall*
*ask of me: 'Do here,*
**in this place** *- the home*
*that you came from - the same*
*as we heard that you did*
*in Capernaum'.*"

Then he went on, in repeating:

"*I say to you, truly,*
*no prophet finds*
*any acceptance **in***
***their home town**. -*

*In the times of Elijah*
*- I promise you - so many*
*widows were there when*
*the skies rained not,*

*for three and half years,*
   *as bitterest famines*
      *reigned all through*
         *the land.* —

*Elijah was sent*
*to a widow in Zarenhath,*
*Sidar - to widows*
*of drought* **was not sent**

*and though many who lived*
*in his Israel suffered*
*with leprosy,*
*this prophet*
*cleansed* **only Naaman**, *a Syrian."*

The congregation were burning
with rage at the words
he spake, —

Jesus found he could
   not perform miracles here
      except laying on hands,
         curing sick
      and infirm.

*He was taken aback*
*at their absolute*
***absence*** *of* FAITH.

Many rose from
their places and
drove Jesus out
of the town —
to the peak
of the hill where it stood.

They intended to hurtle him off
the cliff's edge
- yet he made
his way straight
through the crowd,

and he went on his way.

(M 6:1-6 / Mt 13:53-58 / L 4:14-30)

## 42. "EVEN DEMONS OBEY HIM!"

JESUS WENT WITH HIS GROUP
to Capernaum,
in Galilee —
Sabbath came,
then he went into
the temple; he started to teach.

— All who prayed there
were stunned by the words
that he spoke - for he taught
them as one with authority and
not some mere preacher of Law.

Of a sudden,
   a man in the synagogue,
     - gripped by a spirit unclean -
       cried out **loud**,
      at the top of
      his voice:

*"Go away!*
STAY AWAY FROM ME!

*- and the demon that haunted him **fled**,
for
it had been **forced out***

*What do **you**
want with **US** -
JESUS of Nazareth?
Have you come here to
destroy us completely?
I KNOW WHO YOU ARE -
'HOLY ONE' of GOD!"*

"SILENCE!"

spoke Jesus
both firmly
and sternly:

**"Begone from him now
and returnest not!"**

- Then that man,
he shook violently
till - at one instant -
he gave out a shriek
and the demon that
haunted him *fled*,
         for
it had been *forced out*.

All the people stood
awestruck, stunned,
and they asked of
each other - and
of themselves:

"*Who and what
is this man? And
what **power of words**!
He speaks with authority!*

*Even the demons obey him
— **he orders, they leave**!*"

The stories of good things
that Jesus had done
would spread
all around
Galilee,

    *everywhere else.*


(M 1:21-28 / L 4:31-37)

## 43. A DISCIPLE'S MOTHER CURED

THAT DAY AS THEY
stepped from
the temple
they made their
way over to Simon
and Andrew's home.

Immediately Jesus
was told of the illness
that now beset Simon's
mother-in-law, he parted
the synagogue, James and
John with him to make it
straight out to the house.

When they stepped in
at once it was clear,
Simon's mother
had fever severe.

They all turned toward Jesus
— *in hope of his help.*

So he went to her bedside,
    took hold of her hand;
he leaned over her body,
  the illness drove out,
*— it listened to him*
*and it suddenly left.*
*Simon's mother* **immediately**
        ***got out of bed.***

She got up to her feet
- all the fever was gone -
and she took on her role
as the host of this home.
Yes, the mother-in-law
 of Simon-Peter,
 now waited
 upon them
 the usual way
   — attending to
*everything* Jesus needed,
    or Simon or Andrew
       or any one else.

(M 1:29-31 / Mt 8:14-15 / L 4:38-39)

## 44. THE NEWS OF ALL GALILEE

AS THE DUSK FELL
that evening,
demon-possessed in
their hordes
and the sickly - who
suffered
from various ailments
- were
brought out to Jesus by
villagers,
*eager that he would
heal them.*

Outside the door of
this house gathered
all of the town
and then
Jesus cured *so many*
fraught with afflictions,
he cast out the demons
from those possessed.

He laid hands upon **each,
every one of them**
— drove out the devils with
simply one word :

"*BEGONE!*"

And with that,
ALL WERE CURED
OF THEIR ILLS. —


Yet **never** would Jesus
let demons speak out, –
for they knew *who he was.*

Some would scream at him,
"YOU ARE THE SON OF GOD!"

So, on chasing them out
he would silence
their speeches
as they knew
      HE **was**
           the 'MESSIAH'.

And all that occurred,
          it was fated to be
to fulfill what
          was said through
the prophet
    Isaiah
        who saw in advance:

    "*He takes away illnesses,*
   ***suffers our maladies.***"


(M 1:32-34 / Mt 8:16-17 / L 4:40-41)

## 45. A MOMENT OF SOLITUDE

IN THE EARLIEST HOURS
- while it was still dark -
Jesus got up and left
the house behind him.

As day broke he went
to a quiet place, where
he could be **alone** —
and there Jesus prayed.

The people were searching
to find him
*but they could not find him.*

Simon-Peter and some of
his friends went
in search of their Master.
and finally,
once they had found him,
they shouted out: *"Everyone's
              trying to find you!"*

*As day broke he went to a quiet place, where he could be **alone** — and there Jesus prayed*

*They wanted to make sure
he would not leave them.*

Jesus answered the words
they had spoken,
like this :

*"Then I say to you,
  let us go elsewhere,
  to neighboring villages,
  towns, so I may go and share
  among them the **Good News** of
  the KINGDOM OF GOD — for
  **that is the reason** why
  I have been sent."*

Thus he wandered
through all of Judea and
Galilee, carried on preaching
in all of the synagogues,
demons cast out.

(M 1:35-39 / L 4:42-44)

## IV. NEW TEACHINGS

*Teach the wise, they
shall become wiser —*

*teach the righteous, their
learning shall grow*

PROVERBS 9:9

# 46. "BLESSÈD ARE YE"

JESUS WENT UP
  to a plateau —
    those following
      him were enormous
        in number

— from Judea and
from Jerusalem, also
from coasts around Tyre
  and Sidon, **so many** came out
      to hear him.

Some had come out to be healed
  of illnesses,
    ailments, and others
  long plagued
by demons
  were cleansed of them
      now —
people reached out
  to touch him in knowing
    *his power*
  *could heal* ALL.

He looked upon all of his followers
there — then Jesus spoke
these words:

*"Blessèd are ye
who are poor or
dispirited, yours is
the K*ingdom *of G*od.

*Blessèd are ye
in mourning,
for you shall
be given solace;*

*blessèd are ye who
are now in tears,
for later will
you laugh;*

*blessèd are ye,
the humble,* **you**
*shall be given* A*LL*;

*blessèd are ye who
hunger and thirst for
what is* R*IGHT, for you
shall be satisfied* **soon**;

> "blessèd are ye, the pure in heart,
> for you will see GOD
>          **with your own eyes**"

*blessèd are ye who
show mercy, you
shall be shown
mercy in turn;*

*blessèd are ye,
the pure in heart,
for you will see G*OD
*with **your own eyes**;*

*blessèd are ye who
CREATE ONLY PEACE —
for you shall be called
the 'Children of G*OD*';*

*blessèd are ye when
the **other** despises you,
hurls at you insults,
rebukes you as evil
— all because of
the S*ON *of M*AN.

*Blessèd are ye who
confront persecution
for yours is the quest
for what is right, - yours
is the K*INGDOM *of H*EAVEN."

- Not long after this,
Jesus carried on saying:

"— *Rejoice in this news*
*and exult in that day*
*which is joined by*
**joy transcendent**,
*for GREAT will*
*your prizes*
*in Heaven be.*

*Blessèd are ye when*
*you suffer indignity,*
*slanderous malice,*
*because of me.*

*Forget not*
*how prophets*
*of times of yore —*
***they** faced persecution,*

       *just like you.*"

(Mt 5:1-12 / L 6:17-23)

## 47. "YET WOE TO YE ALL"

"*YET WOE TO YE ALL  
who are wealthy —  
**already** have you  
enjoyed all of  
your comforts.*

*Woe to ye all who  
are fully fed now,  
**later** you will know  
hunger. You shall starve.*

*Woe to ye all who are  
laughing right now;  
**later on** you will weep  
and wail like mourners.*

*Woe to ye, lastly, when all  
speak of you in great eulogies  
just as were counterfeit  
prophets — **adored by your  
forebears** like idols before.*"

(L 6:24-28)

## 48. SALT OF THE EARTH

*"SALT OF THE EARTH*

*are You! —*

*Yet if salt tasted*

*no longer salty —*

*whatever could make*

*it be salty once more?*

*— Salt without flavor*

*is GOOD-FOR-NOTHING,*

*except to throw out*

*and to tread*

*underfoot."*

(Mt 5:13)

# 49. "YOU ARE THE LIGHT OF THE WORLD"

THEN HE SAID TO THEM:

*"When dost thou*
  *bring out a lamp*
  ***then** to hide it away*
  *beneath bed or bowl?*

*Wouldst thou not first*
*place it up on a stand*
*so the flames can be*
*shared all around? -*

*That which was hidden*
*is meant to be* SEEN —
*the **concealed** now*
*placed in the* LIGHT OF DAY.

*What was closed off*
*from our sight **is to***
***be disclosed** -*
*in your eyes now*
NEW REVELATIONS.

*Whoever hath ears*

*to hear me —*

**let them hear**

AND UNDERSTAND!*"*

After saying

all this,

Jesus added:

"*Ponder long on*

*what you hear —*

*about its meaning*

*think at length:*

*as much*

*as you give*

*will be given*

*to you* **and far**

**greater besides**

*for* WHOEVER

MORE POSSESSETH,

**SHALL BE GIVEN MORE,**

*— while those
who haveth not, lo,*
**the little they have
will be taken away**
*from them - ALL
SHALL BE LOST!"*

Detecting that
clouds of confusion
persisted, Jesus
went on, saying:

"*YOU ARE THE LIGHT
OF THE WORLD, I say,
like a town on a hill
you are witnessed by all*
**- and never can fail
to be noticed!**

*Just as none
light a lamp
to entrap in
a jar of clay -*

*no*, that lamp
is placed up on
its stand so that
all in the house from
its flame RECEIVE LIGHT -

likewise, I say
LET THY LIGHT SHINE FORTH
FOR ALL - so that
others may see your **acts
of goodness** -
and so they may glorify
YOU —
OUR FATHER IN HEAVEN."

Another day,
Jesus returned
to this thought:

"*Just as none
light a candle
to trap beneath
a darkened bowl
— but where best
bestows light —*

*to the body, your eye is
a lamp and*
**your body itself is light**

*— yet with eyes unclear
your body seems drowned
in overwhelming night. —*

*Be sure that the light
which is in you*
SHINES FORTH,
*do not let it be
clouded by darkness*

*Your body entire
is light and not dark —*

**You** *can be like that lamp
whose light shines upon you!"*


(M 4:21-25 / Mt 5:14-16 / L 8:16-18; 11:33-36)

## 50. **THE LAW OF THE KINGDOM**

"YE MUST NOT BELIEVE
that I come to destroy
or be done with
the Law or
the Prophets;
I come not **abolishing**
them but to make what they say
                **become true**.

Verily, I say to ye,
until Earth and leaves vanish
not even the tiniest letter
nor one stroke of ink will be taken
from Moses' Law —
NOT TILL ALL IS ACCOMPLISHED.

If someone ignores just
the slightest or smallest
commandment and teaches
to others the same — then
they shall be marked out as
    **the most insignificant** in
       Heaven's Kingdom.

*Whereas those who do teach and*
*do practise each single commandment*
*- no matter how trivial - they shall*
*shine forth as the* **Great Ones**
*in* **that Kingdom***.*

*For I say to you,*

*only your personal*

*actions of* RIGHTEOUSNESS

*can surpass those of the Pharisees*

*and of the teachers of Law;*

*not till then will you*

*find the* **sure path**

*that will lead*

*all the way*

*to the* KINGDOM — *of* **HEAVEN***."*

(Mt 5:17-20)

# 51. 'DO NO MURDER'

"ALL HAVE HEARD
what was said to the populace,
'ere many years:
**Thou shalt do
no murder**: all murderers, they
shall with judgment be faced.'

Yet I say to ye, those who
bear **anger** and **hatred**
'gainst sister or brother,
shall face judgment too.

And also, whoever says
**Raca**\* to brother or sister
shall answer their charges
in court; and beyond that:

those who mock others
as 'Imbecile!', 'Idiot!'
teeter on the rim of
Hell's blazing abyss.

---

\* This Hebrew word has a meaning similar to 'brainless fool' in English

*For this reason then, if thou art
giving thy gift at the altar
and know that your
brother or sister
hold grudges
against you -
abandon your gift
at that altar and **first go
be reconciled with them** —*
ONLY AFTER *return to thy offering.*

*Resolve matters rapidly with
thy opponents
— who take you to court.*

*Settle matters whilst you
make your way to the court
or beware that your enemy send
you straight into the bailiff's hands
— who shall throw you then
into your prison cell.*

***Verily**, I say to thee, that
thou shalt not be free
till each last cent be paid back."*

(Mt 5:21-26)

## 52. REGARDING ADULTERY

"YE HAVE HEARD
the commandment
that has been laid down:

'— **Thou shalt not
commit adultery**',

- yet I say, those
who are gazing
with lust have
committed it
**already** in their hearts.

If your right eye
should cause you
to stumble, then
skewer it out and
throw it aside – for
it does you more good
to lose part of your body
than all of it thrown
in the fires of Hell.

*And again, if
your right hand
should make you
lose balance, then
cut it off also and
throw it away.*

*It will do you
more good to lose
part of your body
— in place of
the whole
being
thrown into Hell."*

(Mt 5:27-30)

## 53. A WORD ON DIVORCE

"YE HAVE HEARD
what was said, that:

'Whoever divorces
their wife shall
provide
a certificate
to her, proving this',

yet I say that
whoever divorces
their wife when it
does not occur due
to carnal sin, —

coerces her into
adultery,
forcing
that sin on
whoe'er remarries her."

(Mt 5:31-32)

## 54. "SWEAR NO OATHS"

"*EVEN BEYOND THAT,*
*you know*
*it was said*
*to us long ago:*

**'Break not thy oath;**
*you must honor*
*the oaths that*
*you make to*
*the* LORD'.

*Yet I say to you -*
**swear not one oath**
        **whatsoever:**
*not by Heaven*
*(for that is God's throne),*
*nor by Earth - which is like*
        *His footstool -*
*and nor by Jerusalem even,*
        *for that is*
*the Great King's town.*

*Apart from that,*
*do not swear*
**even**
*upon your own head*

*because you could not*
*turn*
*even one*
*strand of your*
*own hair white or black.*

*Nothing more*
*need to be said*
*except '****Yes****' or '****No****' –*

*for whatever you say*
*beyond that,*
*it derives*
*from*
*the devil alone!"*

(Mt 5:33-37)

# 55. 'AN EYE FOR AN EYE'?

*"WHAT WAS SAID
before, all of you
know very well:
'AN EYE FOR AN EYE,
A TOOTH FOR A TOOTH'*

*— yet I say to you,*
**fight not the wicked.**

*If someone should
strike you across
the right cheek,
then offer to them
your left one as well,
and
if anyone ever should
sue you - and* **even
your shirt** *has
been granted in
settlement - then I say,*
**offer your coat as well.**

*If someone should force*
*you to go with them*
**one mile** —
*then, I say,*
*offer to go with them* **two**.

**Provide** *unto those who*
*request of you*
*anything,*
*and if*
*one asks*
*you to lend*
*them* **whatever**
THEN TURN THEM NOT AWAY."


(Mt 5:38-42)

## 56. "LOVE THY ENEMIES"

*"NONE OF YOU  
**are unaware** of  
the saying — to  
'Love thy neighbor  
and hate thy enemy'.*

*Yet I say to all of you  
here who are listening:  
those who hate you and  
**even** your enemies* LOVE,  
*those who curse you,* BLESS,  
*and the ones who oppress  
you and treat you bad  
—* PRAY FOR THEM  
*and in that way  
become children  
of GOD - your Father  
of mercy in Heaven above.*

*Does somebody **slap** you  
in the face? - then offer to them  
        your other cheek.*

*Does someone steal*
*your coat from you? - then*
***give*** *them the shirt off your back.*

*To all who request of you,* ***give***
*and if someone takes*
*that which is yours*
*—* ***let it go*** *and*
***don't ever demand it back.***

*Also, act toward others*
***as you would***
***have them treat you too.***

*It is true that the Lord*
*lets His Sun dawn on*
EVIL *and* GOOD,
*— that*
*it rains on*
***unrighteous***
*and* ***righteous*** *alike.*

*But if you return love just to*
*those who love you, then* ***how***
***does that actually merit reward?***

*— Even sinners,
collectors of taxes, do that!*

*And if all that
you do is to greet
your own people then
how are you **better**
than anyone else?*

*If you do good to
who treat you well:
tell me please, **whatever
is special in that**? —*

*And if you have extended
a loan to another, expecting
that it shall be repaid, tell me
**what good have you done at all**?*

*Even criminals lend to their own,
even sinners expect
to get back
every pound
that they lend.*

*I repeat,*
**love your enemies**,
    *treat them kind and*
*lend money to them*
    *not expecting it back.*

*In that case,*
    *your prize in the end*
        *will be great and*
    *you shall become*
    *children of GOD*
*on High.*

*He is kind*
*to the ones without gratitude too*
*and to those*
*who act only with malice dark.*

*— Therefore*
*aim for* **perfection**
*in just the same way as*
*your Heavenly Father*
*Himself is* **perfect**.*"*

(Mt 5:43-48 / L 6:27-36)

## 57. THE MEANING OF 'RIGHTEOUSNESS'

*"REGARDING THE PRACTICE
of 'Righteousness',
make not a show
of it, just to be seen.*

*If you act in this way
then thy Father in Heaven
shall give no reward.*

*Therefore,
when you donate
to the poor, do not do so
with fanfare and boasts
- like hypocrites out
in the temples
or streets -
just for
honor and praise.*

*In all truth, I say,
do not allow your left hand
to know that which
your right hand is doing —*

***that way**, your giving*
*may take place*
*in secret.*

*Only then*
*may your Father -*
*who sees even secrets*
*- give YOU the reward*
*that you **truly***
***deserve.**"*

(Mt 6:1-5)

## 58. "OUR FATHER, WHO ART IN HEAVEN"

JESUS, HE WAS PRAYING
in an isolated place
that day —
as soon as
he had finished,
one of his disciples asked:

"*Lord please teach us,* **teach
us how to pray**,
*as John has shown his own.*"

And Jesus answered:

"*When you pray
then just say* **this** —
"OUR FATHER
WHO ART IN HEAVEN,
HALLOWED BE
THY NAME.
THY KINGDOM COME,
MAY THY WILL BE DONE
ON EARTH,
AS IT IS IN HEAVEN.

GIVE US THIS DAY,
  OUR DAILY BREAD.
FORGIVE US OUR DEBTS OF SIN
    AS WE ALSO FORGIVE
EVERY ONE WHO SINS AGAINST US.
  — LASTLY, LEAD US
      NOT INTO
        TEMPTATION
  BUT DELIVER US FROM EVIL."

Then Jesus provided
this extra advice:

"*When you pray,
then I say
do not do so
like hypocrites,
standing so proud
in the temples and out
on street corners
– in order that
they shall be
witnessed
by all.*

*Listen to them with*
*their bustling verbosity,*
*thinking a wealth of words*
*will ensure that they are heard.*

*Honestly,*
*I say to you,*
*these have already*
*gained their full reward.*

*When it is time*
*for you to pray,*
*then go off*
*to your room,*
*shut the door and*
*make prayers to your Father*
                       *— **unseen**.*

*In this way,*
*the Father, who*
*sees you in secret —*
*will give you your proper*
                       *reward.*

There is
no need to act
like the hypocrites do
— for your Father
knows all that
you need
**in advance of**
**your even asking.**

Understand
that exactly as you
forgive those who have
sinned against you,
your Father in
Heaven
YOUR SINS
**shall forgive.**
If you show not
forgiveness to others,
       — the FATHER
**shall not forgive** your sins."

(Mt 6:5-15 / L 11:1-4)

## 59. "YOUR FATHER SEES WHAT IS UNSEEN"

"WHEN THERE IS FASTING,
do not act so somberly
just like a hypocrite,
pulling such faces
and grimacing,
showing off
all of the pain
that you suffer
for what you endure.

Truly, I tell you,
they've already had
their **full reward**

No, when time comes
for fasting,
then first cut your hair,
also freshen
your face so that no-one
can tell
that thou art in a fast.

*Only your Father
above will know -*
**who no-one sees.**

*And your Father,*
**who sees even
what is
unseen**, *will
remunerate you
for what you are doing."*

(Mt 6:16-18)

## 60. TREASURES IN HEAVEN

*"DO NOT HOARD*
*all your precious*
*belongings in*
*this world*
*for rodents*
*and pests will*
*destroy them or*
*thieves may steal in,*
**robbing you of them all.**

*Instead, collect treasure*
*in Heaven, — where*
*rodents and pests*
*cannot ruin it,*
*somewhere*
*that no thieves*
*can break in and steal.*

*Where your true treasures are,*
**there will thy true heart**
*be also."*

(Mt 6:19-21)

## 61. "BEWARE DARKNESS WITHIN"

*"REMEMBER THE EYES
are the light of
the body,
- for
if they
are healthy,
your body entire
will shine with LIGHT.*

*However,
if eyes are
poor in sight,
then your body
seems shrouded —
in pitch black* **night**.

*If the light within you
itself should be
darkness, —*
**beware, o beware of
how great is that darkness!"**

(Mt 6:22-23)

## 62. **GOD AND MAMMON**

NO PERSON CAN SERVE
two different masters.

— On one hand,
you will despise
one of the two;

on the other,
you dedicate love
to the one,
while so hating
        the other.

— Hear me,
You cannot serve
Mammon* and God
at the self-same time."

(Mt 6:24)

\* *Money* or *Wealth* as a false god

## 63. WISDOM FOR TOMORROW

*"I SAY TO YOU NOW,*
*about your life*
**fret not —**
*what you eat -*
*what you drink -*
*what your body requires*
        *- and what you earn.*

*Life's about more than*
*just food and drink!*

*Is the body not more*
*than*
*the garments it wears?*

*— Open your eyes to*
*the birds of the skies,*
*who nor reap nor sow*
*nor store up their food;*

*yet, in spite of that fact,*
*doth your Father in Heaven*
        *look after them well.*

*And YOU,
are you not
of more value
than **them**?*

*Yet can even
a single among you
add one
single hour of time
to your lives
through your fretting
and worrying so? —*

*Then again, also,
why do you fuss
about clothes?*

*Cast your eyes
on the flowers that
grow in the fields —*

*they do no hard work,
and they spin no clothes
— yet I say to you now*

*that nor even* SOLOMON
*clad in magnificence*
**equals**
**a single one of them**.

*Simply ask yourself this:*
*if God clothes plants*
*that grow from*
*the earth —*
*growing*
*one day then*
*on bonfires burnt,*
*will the Father not also*
*make sure you are clothed?*

*— ye of such* **meager faith**!

*Leave off your worrying,*
*griping and asking:*

"What have we to eat?"
**and**
"What have we to drink?"
**and**
"How will we be clothed?"

*- Only unbelievers
believe in these worries,
while your Lord, above,
He knows all that
you need.*

*However,
you first must
**seek out** his Kingdom,
acquire your righteousness
– then, all you wish for
will follow from that.*

*Thus, do not worry
  about the morrow -
    tomorrow can worry
        about itself.*

*Every day, I say,
  has enough
    trouble  alone."*

(Mt 6:25-34)

# 64. 'JUDGE AND BE JUDGED'

"JUDGE NOT then also
thou shalt not be judged;

for in just the same way
you make judgment
of others, you shall find
that you yourself are judged.

Condemn not and then
you will
not be condemned.

Forgive and you
too
shall be forgiven. —

Give, and to you
will
be given also,

full measures,
compressed just as tight as can be,
brimming over and
spilling right into your lap.

*— For with just
the same measure
you use for others
shall things be
measured out
for you. —"*

*And now
why do you stare at
a mere speck of sawdust
in thy brother's eye,
and dare say
to him:*

    *'I must, O brother,
      take dust from your eye',*

*- while you see not
a plank
that juts
out from your own?*

*Thou, o* **hypocrite supreme** *-*
LYING TO THYSELF AND OTHERS*!*

*Take out the plank from*
*thine own eye first*
*and then*
*maybe*
*you'll see*
*how you can*
*remove dust from*
*your brother's eye too!*

*Do not give to the hounds*
*what is sacred to man,*
*nor throw pearls that*
*you own, to the swine.*
*If you do so, then all that*
*was thrown may be trampled*
   BENEATH THEIR FEET —
*    and*
*   they  shall*
*  turn  and  tear*
*you   to   pieces.*


(Mt 7:1-6 / L 6:37-38; L 6:41-42)

## 65. **BLIND LEADING BLIND**

JESUS LIKED TO RELATE
this brief parable
also:

"*How can a blind man
lead one who is blind?*

*— will they not then
both fall in a pit?*

*The pupil is not
placed above
the tutor
yet all
who are
fully instructed
will end up becoming
as wise as their teachers too.*

(L 6:39-40)

# 66. "ASK AND IT SHALL BE GIVEN TO YOU"

"REQUEST IT
and
it shall be given to you;

knock on the door
and
it will be opened.

For all who request,
**receive**;
they who seek shall find
and to one
who knocks at the door -
**that door**
**shall be opened** to them.

What parent among you,
if ever
your son
request bread,
would provide him
        a piece
           of **rock**?

*Or if he made
   a wish for
      some fish,
would give him
         a **serpent**
            instead?*

*    Or a **scorpion** to
his request for an egg?*

*If <u>you</u> then - evil though
you be - know how to give
good things to thy children
— how much more will
thy Heavenly Father
gift good things
to those who
ask of HIM!*

*— How much more,
imagine then,
does He
give HOLY SPIRIT
to those who request it."*

*Therefore,
in all things,*
**do unto others**
AS YOU WOULD HAVE
THEM DO UNTO YOU —

*that is the essence
of **all** the* LAW *and
of the* PROPHETS *too."*

- At that juncture,
Jesus related a story:

*" — Just suppose you have
a friend, to whom you go
one night at midnight,
and to him you say:*

*'O Friend of mine, please
would you lend me
just three loaves
tonight -
for **another**
**friend** is visiting but
my own cupboard's* BARE.'

*Now let us suppose*
*that the one in his home*
*says: 'Go away, the door's been*
    *locked, my family are*
    *all in bed, and*
    *there's no way*
    *you can come in,*
**I cannot give you anything.***'*

*I say to you,*
*he does not get up*
*and lend to you, because*
*you were friends, but*

*only because you were*
*shamefully bold - he will*
*certainly get out of bed and*
*give all that you ask for.*

*Therefore, I say*
*this to you:* **Ask and it will**
    **be given to you.**
**Seek and you shall find.**

**Knock at the door
and it will be
opened.**

*For everyone who asks,*

*receives;*

*who seeks, finds —*

*and to*

*they who knock,*

*the door,      it shall*

*be            opened.*

(Mt 7:7-12 / L 11:5-12)

## 67. 'NARROW IS THE GATE'

"ENTER THROUGH
the narrow gate,
for the gate
that is wide
and the road
that is broad
will bring you to
absolute ruination,

— and many are they
who go through that gate.

Narrow, however, the gate
and slender the road
that can take you
to LIFE itself -
and few are
the souls who find it."

(Mt 7:13-14)

## 68. TRUE AND FALSE PROPHETS

"BEWARE OF FALSE PROPHETS,
they come in sheep's clothing
yet underneath they are
like rabid wolves. —

You will recognize
them by the fruit they offer.

Who would pick grapes
from the briars
or figs from where
thistles and thorns are found?

In the same way, a good tree
bears good fruit while
bad trees bear
only bad fruit.

A good tree
can **not** bear bad fruit

and a bad one
can offer **none good**.

*— Just as each tree that
bears not good fruit
is hacked down
and thrown
into the fire,*

*- the same way
shall you also recognize
their fruit by **what they are.**"*


(Mt 7:15-20)

# 69. WHAT THE MOUTH SPEAKS

"A GOOD PERSON has good things
stored in their heart
and from this
they are able to make what is good,

while an evil one gathers up
only the darkness
in their heart,
from whence comes evil alone.

The TONGUE,
**it releases what
fills someone's heart.**"

(L 6:43-45)

# 70. TRUE AND FALSE DISCIPLES

*"IT IS NOT EACH*
*who calls to me*

**'Lord, o Lord'**

*who shall enter*
*the Kingdom,*

*but only the ones*
*who fulfill the will*
*of my Father, who*
*lives in Heaven.*

*Many are those*
*who will say to me,*
*when the day comes:*

*'Lord, o Lord,*
*in your name*
*we were prophets*
*and in your name*
*we did* **such** *miracles -*
*and in your own name*
*we drove out demons.'*

*And to them,*
*I will plainly say:*

**'Never have I even**
    **known you,**
**begone**
    **from me,**
**agents of Evil!**
        **BEGONE!'"**

(Mt 7:21-23)

## 71. 'LIKE A HOUSE BUILT ON ROCK'

*"I HEAR YOU CALL OUT*

*'O Lord, o Lord'*

*yet ignoring my words,*
　*doing not what I say.*

*As for all those who*
*come to me -*
*hearing my words*
*and enacting*
*their meaning - I say*
*to you this:*

*those who listen and*
*follow me are like the wise*
*one who builds*
*their house on sturdy rock -*
*with foundations*
*dug under it, deep beneath.*

*As hard rains pour and*
*stream banks swell and*
*winds blow wild and*
*whip right against it,*

*this house shall not fall,*
*no matter how harsh*
*be the storms that strike,*
*for this dwelling is*
*set upon* **solid rock**.

*However, those who hear*
*these words*
*yet dismiss my advice*
*in real life,*
*is like a fool who builds*
*their home*
*on no foundations,*
 *shifting sands.*

*As hard rains pour and*
*stream banks swell and*
*winds blow wild and*
*whip against it —*
 *down it tumbles*
 *in an instant,*
 NOTHING LEFT.*"*

(Mt 7:24-27 / L 6:46-49)

## 72. "TELL NO-ONE OF THIS"

AS JESUS CONCLUDED
his teachings that day,
the crowds there
were stunned
by the things he explained

- for he taught them as one
with command and authority,
not like the teachers of Law
      they had known.

When Jesus descended
the side of the mountain,
huge masses of people
were following him.

Once town was reached
then
a leper came up to him —
covered
with lesions from head to toe.

He fell to his knees
and of Jesus implored:

"O Lord, **if thou willest it**,
   *thou canst cleanse me.*"

Jesus, annoyed at these words,
all the same reached
his hands forth to
touch him, in saying: "*I will it.*
   NOW BE THOU CLEAN!"

Instantaneously,
he was **no more a leper**
  — *his body was purified*
      OF ALL SINS.
The leprosy left him.
    *He was* CURED.

- Yet when
Jesus was sending
this man on his way,
he commanded:
     "*Tell no-one
    of what happened here!* -

*No, do not speak to anyone.*
*— **No-one can know!***

*Only go to thy rabbi and
bare him your body - show
**you have been cured** - then
pay tribute to Moses as it was
ordained - because you
have been cleansed
— in testimony
of the* L*ORD*.*"*

But alas, just as soon
  as the leper had left,
    this one went around
      everywhere —
  spreading the news
of what Jesus had done.

And the word
  spread so quickly
    that no-one could
      stop it: all heard
    that this leper
by Jesus *was cleansed.*

It was due to this
  Jesus could not
    travel freely,
      requiring
        to rest
          in
            the quietest
              regions

*away from the crowds*

    But though
    Jesus went far
from the populace,
praying there,

people still
  came out
    to find him,
      arriving from
        near and wide.

(M 1:40-45 / Mt 7:28-8:4 / L 5:12-1)

# V. <u>A NEW CALLING</u>

*The Lord said to Abraham:*

"*LEAVE NOW YOUR COUNTRY,*
*YOUR HOUSE AND PEOPLE -*
*THEN GO TO THE LAND*
*I SHALL SHOW **YOU**.*"

## 73. A SIGN OF FISH

ONE DAY, JESUS WAS
stood by
the lake of Gennesaret -
people
were crowding around as
he spoke
the 'WORD OF GOD'.

At the shore
of the waters
Jesus saw: a pair
of boats left there
by fishermen —
nets being
washed.

So he stepped onto
one of the two
- which was
Simon's;
he asked if
they could go
a little way out.

*So he stepped onto one of the two
- which was Simon's;
he asked if
they could go a little way out*

- Jesus sat down on board
 and he preached to
 the people who
 were on shore.

When he paused from
his teaching,
he then said to Simon:

*"Now take us
out deep in the waters and
cast out our nets to catch
some fish."*

To this, Simon
answered: *"We've
toiled all night, Master,
yet we have not caught*
 **one single fish.**

*But if you insist,
 I will cast out the nets
 one more time —*
  **just as you ask."**

After this had been done,
such a great mass of fish
were caught up in the nets
— **they began to break.**

When that happened
they signalled to men
in another craft: *help
was required* — they
came right on over.

When both of the vessels
were filled up so full that
*the pair of them, both
were about to sink -*

then Simon (called
Peter) **he saw this**
and dropped to
the floor on
his knees
before Jesus
and cried out:

*"Abandon me Lord,*
***I am filled with sin!"***

*Simon and every companion of theirs were extremely amazed at the wondrous catch*

Simon and every
companion of theirs
were extremely amazed
at the wondrous catch,
as were James and John -
of Zebedee sons - who were
part of the crew that day.

Upon hearing his words,
Jesus looked at Simon
and said: "**Be not
in fear**, *– from
this day forth
thou shalt fish
for people instead.*"

- After that,
they tethered
their boats ashore,
left everything there

— *followed after Jesus.*

(L 5:1-11)

# 74. **THE MIRACLE OF FORGIVENESS**

SOME DAYS AFTERWARD
Jesus returned to
Capernaum -
his childhood town.

Of course, people
got word
that he had returned
home and
they crowded round,
outside his door,
     massing up
    in their throngs,
there was *no room*
*to move.*

People came from Judea,
    Jerusalem too,
  from each
village in Galilee,

*see and hear* Jesus.

Although there was no space
*still* Jesus taught them
— with Pharisees,
teachers of law, in attendance.

The power of God seemed
to rest upon Jesus -
the sick were brought
out to him,
that they be cured.

A group of four men
came,
a mat held above them,
a one
who was paralyzed laying
upon it —
they carried him forwards,
intending to take him
in Jesus's house,
to present him
*to heal.*

But because of the crowds
all round Jesus,
they just could not reach him,
each way to
his house was blocked off —

so they went on the roof
of that dwelling -
direct above
Jesus - and
dug out
a hole
between tiles,
then lowered him down
through the gap they had made.

Down and down did they
lower him, down
in the midst
of the populace,
down till right there
before Jesus he was -  in front of
                      his eyes.

Perceiving how strong
>was their faith,
to the paralyzed one
>Jesus said:

*"Blessèd be thou, my son*
>*— **all thy sins***
>***are forgiven.**"*

On hearing this,
experts in Law and
some Pharisees sitting
there, started to think
in these ways:

*"Why*
*does this one*
*before us speak thus? - as*
*if God gave such power to **man**!*

*What this rabbi proclaims —*
>*it blasphemes the* Law*!*

*Because* none except *God **can***
>***forgive** human sin!"*

Jesus, inside his mind
instantly sensed
what these people were
thinking, dark in their hearts;

so, responding to *this*
        he asked:

*"Really? But why do you*
    *think such thoughts?*
      *What is easier for*
        *me to say*
          *to him?*

   *Should I say, 'Son,*
**thy sins are forgiven**',
*or should I say:*
*'Get to your feet,*
   *grab your mat*
     *and* ***walk***'?

   *Let me tell you*
  *what **you need***
  ***to know** right now:*

*HE who comes here as*
'SON OF MAN' — HE *can cleanse sin.*

*Yes, the Son of Man comes here - to Earth - with Authority, Absolute: EVEN SIN HE FORGIVES."*

Then he spoke to the paralysed one, saying: *"Get up and walk! Yes, I tell thee — **get up with thy mat and go back to thine home**, RIGHT NOW!"*

Straight away the man got to his feet before all of them, picked up the mat he had lain on, **walked** *home* and thanked GOD — *right up to the skies.*

Everyone saw

and *in awe,*
OVERWHELMED,
made full praise to
God also, said:
"***Never
before*** have we witnessed
such things!"


(M 2:1-12 / Mt 9:2-8 / L 5:17-26)

## 75. DINING WITH SINNERS

ON THE SHORE
of the lake
Jesus stayed and
so many assembled
— *he taught again.*

And once he had
finished,
departing that place,
he saw Levi
- of Alphæus son -
who by some
was called *Matthew*.

- A collector of taxes,
he sat at his stand like
the other collectors,
but Jesus called out:

"Come, **follow me** —
yes, come along with me!
                      *Follow!*"

Hearing this, Levi got up
and left
all things behind him —
          walked
straight after Jesus,
    *at once.*

Soon after, he hosted
the finest of banquets
- for Jesus - at his home.

While Jesus was dining
at Matthew's, he ate
beside other
collectors
of taxes -
*'deplorables'* -
followers also,
they ate with him too.

*Then* it was, teachers of
Law and some Pharisees
- part of their order -
began to complain:

"*How can Jesus,*
    *your Master,*
        *dine here*
    *with such people?*
*with sinners and bailiffs,*
            *collectors of tax?"*

Overhearing this,
Jesus replied to his critics:

"*It is not*
  *the healthy who*
  *most need the doctor*
  *but those who are*
  *sick,* **who still**
  **need to be**
  **cured.**

  *I am not*
  *here for those*
  *who live righteously,*
          SINNERS
     *I come for —*
*to offer* **repentance.**

*Go off and discover  
the meaning  
of this:* 'MY  
WISH IS  
FOR MERCY,  
NOT SACRIFICE' -

*I am come  
to cure sinners —  
**not** those who are healed.*"


(M 2:13-17 / Mt 9:9-13 / L 5:27-32)

# 76. A QUESTION OF FASTING

PHARISEES, LEVITES,
disciples of John,
they were fasting when
what followed next occurred.

Some of John's followers
came up to Jesus,
and asked:

"*How come **our** brethren*
*fast and pray, as*
*do Pharisees,*
*yet yours keep on*
***eating and drinking?***"

To which Jesus replied:

"*So tell me then, can you*
*you force friends of*
*the bridegroom to fast*
*while he is still there?*
*- No, they **cannot do this**,*
*not as long as the groom is alive.*

*Later on,
there will
come a day
when the groom,
he shall be taken from
them: in those days, only
**then** shall there be any fasting."*

Also, he said to them,
just like a parable:

*"No-one repairs
an old garment with
pieces of unshrunk cloth -*

*When a new piece of cloth
is sewn into an old one,
the new piece will shrink
then the garment will tear
   — and the damage
      be worse.*

**New** *does not
         match with* **Old***.*

*- Plus, who pours new wine
into wineskins far older? For
new wine will make old skins
burst apart, new wine will
spill — the skins be ruined.*

*Know that
new wine goes
only in wineskins new,*

*for then both will do well
and be fully preserved.*


**Also**, *who
　　after vintage wine
　　　　wants to drink new?*

*All say, "Old wine, it is
　　**so much finer** than new."*


(M 2:18-22 / Mt 9:14-17 / L 5:33-39)

# 77. 'SOMEWHERE GREATER THAN A TEMPLE'

UPON A SABBATH,
Jesus led disciples on
through fields of corn;

walking beside him,
they were hungry,
so they picked some
ears of maize and
rubbed them in their
fingers, chewed the grain.

Some Pharisees who noticed,
said to Jesus: "**Look here!** Why do
>your disciples break
>the Law — what it
>OUTRIGHT FORBIDS
>on the **Sabbath**?"

So Jesus responded:

"*Have you not read
of the deeds of David,
when he and his friends
were entirely starving?* —

Some Pharisees who noticed, said to Jesus: "**Look here!** Why do your disciples break the Law?"

*In the days of the High Priest Abiathar,
David went into the House of God
and ate the consecrated bread, -
that which only the priests may do
          — according to the L*AW*.*

*To his friends did
    he also give bread and
        he said to them:*

*'Sabbath for Man was created,
  not Man for the Sabbath —
    the* SON OF MAN *even is*
      **Lord of the Sabbath.**'

*Again, have you not read in
        Books of Moses that
priests, while performing
      their synagogue duties,
they violate Sabbath, —
        yet **free of all blame**?*

Somewhere greater
    than a temple
        is at issue here.

*If you understood the words*
    'I WISH FOR MERCY,
        NOT FOR SACRIFICE'
*you would not blame*
*the blameless —*
SON OF MAN,
*Lord of the Temple.*"

And Jesus repeated:

"*The* SON OF MAN *is*
**Lord of the Sabbath.**"

(M 2:23-28 / Mt 12:1-8 / L 6:1-5)

# 78. "STRETCH OUT THY HAND!"

ANOTHER TIME
- a different Sabbath -
Jesus went into a temple,

there he preached until
a man stepped forth —
his right hand *lifeless*.

        - Pharisees,
    teachers of Law
and some others sought
criminal charges to
bring against
*Jesus* -
watching
him closely and
wishing to see him
perform a cure here,
— on the *Sabbath day*.

One of them asked him in
aiming to catch him out:

*"Tell us now, Rabbi,
does Moses' Law
sanction a healing
performed on
the **Sabbath day**?"*

Perceiving
how they were
all thinking within,
Jesus called to the man
with the frail hand:

*"Stand up and step forth
before thy people."*

- So the man stood up,
then
he stepped before them —
and
Jesus turned to all and said:

"I ask, on the Sabbath,
**which one is more lawful**
— do good or do evil?
save life or destroy it?"

"Then what would you do,
 any one of you, if, on the Sabbath,
 a sheep of yours fell in a pit? —"

Every tongue was still.

*He saw rage in their hearts
and was deeply disturbed by
their cold hollow souls.* —

Jesus then asked
        another question :

*" - Then what would you do,
any one of you, if, on the Sabbath,
a sheep of yours fell in a pit?*

*Would you not
grasp your hands round it
- picking your sheep right
out of that pit?*

**Are not people
of far greater value
than sheep!**

*Is it not thus in
accord with* **the L**<sub>AW</sub>
*to do good on the Sabbath?"*

Surveying the people
all round him,
he turned to the man
    and then said:

*"Stretch forth thy hand!"* —

The man stretched out his hand
and the whole of it then
was *restored*, just as good as new.


Levites and Pharisees
burned in their fury,
stormed off from
  the synagogue,
    working out how
      they could scheme
        with Herodians —

    *have Jesus* **killed***.*

(M 3:1-6 / Mt 12:9-14 / L 6:6-11)

# 79. A MULTIPLICATION OF FOLLOWERS

OUT TO THE LAKE
Jesus brought
his disciples
and many
crowds came
there from Galilee too.

On hearing of wonders
that
he was performing,
hordes
came from Judea
and
Idurea, Jerusalem too.

They came
from the regions round
Sidon and
Tyre; they came from
the far side
of Jordan's waters.

Due to the masses of
people,
he asked his disciples
to have
a small boat at the ready
- for this
would prevent him from
being crushed.

Jesus had healed *so many*
that those
who were ill with diseases,
they pushed
to the front just in order to
touch him.

When those
by dark spirits
possessed noticed
Jesus, they fell to
the ground,
yelling:

"*Thou art
the Son of G*OD" —

though he sternly rebuked them,
*to tell no-one else*
*of this.*

Conscious
  the Pharisees
    plotted his downfall,
        Jesus withdrew
          from the temples,
        yet people in masses
        still followed on after him.

  All who were ill
  did he heal but
  warned them:
  *"Do not say a word!"*


(M 3:7-12)

## 80. 'MY SPIRIT UPON HIM'

ALL THAT HAS HAPPENED
   fulfilleth the words
      of Isaiah, the prophet:

*'Behold my servant,*
*my Chosen One,*
*whom I love and*
*in whom I rejoice.*
*upon him I bestow*
*my Spirit, and he shall*
*announce to the World*
*what* **True Justice** *is. —*

*He shall not fight and row*
*or yell - in the streets*
*his voice is silent.*
*He shall not snap*
*an injured reed, or*
*smother a dying flame,*
*not till Justice* **is triumphant.**
*In his name do all people have faith.'*

(Mt 12:15-21)

## 81. "I NAME YE TWELVE"

UPON ONE OF THESE DAYS
Jesus went up
the side of a mountain
and all night
spent praying to God.

When dawn broke then
he called
his disciples up there
- those
he wanted to see.

And from them
he chose twelve who
would be his *apostles*,
to send forth and preach
      the Good News.

    He appointed them
so as to work alongside him
and gave them the powers to
      *exorcize*.

The ones he appointed were:

Simon (whom Jesus
named 'Peter') and
Andrew, his brother,

plus James and John -
of Zebedee sons - whom
together he called *Boaneges*,
    "*the sons of thunder*".

Also Philip,
Bartholomew,
Matthew and Thomas,
James (son of Alphæus),
Thaddæus, Simon the Zealot,

and finally

Judas Iscariot —
he who
would Jesus,
his master, *betray*.

(M 3:13-19 / L 6:12-16)

## 82. DANCING WITH THE DEVIL

JESUS WENT INSIDE A HOUSE
and once again great crowds
assembled; neither he
nor his disciples
could even stop and eat.

When his family heard what
was happening,
they went to Jesus, in saying:
"*It's crazy to
let things get so out of hand!*"

It was then that a man plagued by demons
was brought out before him
— a man who was
blind and mute.

*Jesus drove
out the demons.*

*The man **saw** and **spoke**.*

"NO, 'tis only Beelzebub,
Prince of **all** demons,
by whose power
this one exorcizes"

All those present were stunned, asking:

"Is this one **truly** the Son of David?"

— All the while
Jesus was tested by
people who wished
to have *signs* that
his works were
DIVINE.

Experts in law
from Jerusalem —
Pharisees too — heard
what people were saying
of 'David', and some
answered thus:

"NO, 'tis only Beelzebub,
Prince of **all** demons,
by whose power
this one exorcizes,

for HE is **possessed**.

Jesus could even hear
what they were thinking
and called them all over
to answer their thoughts,
speaking parables now:

*"An empire split or*
*a kingdom divided*
*against itself shall*
*only fall into ruin.*

*- Likewise a city or*
*home divided* ***inside***
*cannot stand.* THEY
CANNOT SURVIVE.

*So how is it* ***Satan might***
***drive out Satan?*** *—*
*Opposing himself*
***he could not stand!***

*At odds with himself,*
*in division, his kingdom*
*would fall* — HIS DEMISE
      WOULD BE NIGH*!*

*— I say this as
all of you claim that
I cast out in Beelzebub's*

                        *name.*

***If*** *- as you say - I drive
out through* **his powers**, *then
just by whose powers do*
**you** *expel spirits? —*

If by POWERS OF SATAN
then you shall become
your own judges too!

However, if it is
through **Spirit Divine**
that I exorcize demons -
with part of the Hand
of GOD - is it not true
HIS KINGDOM
is **now** and
**already**
           upon YOU?

*— Somebody built  
like a strongman and armed  
at the ready, protecting his home:  
his belongings are **safe**.*

*In point of fact,  
no-one can barge in  
his house unless bound up first!  
**Only then** can his home  
be plundered. —*

*When somebody stronger  
breaks through his defences,  
suppresses his arms (in which  
**he put all trust**) then everything  
will be stripped from him — and  
all his possessions shared out."*

Jesus then heard them say  
this of him,  
'he has a spirit impure',

thus he also said this:

"*Verily, I say to you, may* **anyone** *be pardoned* ALL THEIR SINS, — *for each foul word they write or say;*

*whoever speaks ill of the* SON OF MAN **shall be forgiven.**

*But whoever blasphemes* GOD'S SPIRIT **ne'er shall be forgiven** *- not in this age or in eras to come, for in doing so, they bear the* **weight** *of Eternal Sin .*

*Whoever is not standing with me, fights against me — whoever does not gather with me,* SCATTERS FAR APART."

(M 3:20-30 / Mt 12:22-32 / L 11:14-23)

# 83. A NOTE UPON DEMONS AND A BLESSING

BEFORE LEAVING THE TEMPLE,
he added as well: "***Make sure***
*after a demon departs*
*someone's person,*
*it travels through*
*desolate zones -*
*that it seeks rest*
**but** DOES NOT ATTAIN THIS.

*Following lack of success*
*in achieving this, then*
*it shall say to itself:*
*'In that case, I'll go back*
*to the* **house that I left!**'

*And if, on arriving, it finds*
*that its house of before*
*is swept clean and is*
*pristine, in order, then*
*off it will go to get seven*
*more spirits,* ***more evil by far***
*and with them it shall go back to*
*wreak **greater havoc** — set up*
                     *a* NEW HOME*!*

*Therefore, after all,
shall the state of
the exorcized one
be in fact even worse
than it was at the first!"*

As Jesus was speaking
upon these topics,
a woman called
out to him
from the crowd:

"*Blessèd be she who
has birthed thee
and nursed thee*",

to which Jesus
answered:

"*No -* **blessèd are
those who attend
to the voice of God
and His words obey.**"

(L 11:24-28)

# 84. "MY MOTHER AND MY BROTHERS"

JESUS WAS PREACHING
inside the house,
and the masses
were gathered
on every side.

Brothers and mother
of Jesus arrived at
the dwelling —
*through crowds*
*could not reach*
*him at all —*

they waited OUTSIDE
by the door as they wanted
to speak with him **now**.

- They sent someone in to
tell Jesus that they had arrived
and awaited him there. —

The message was taken
inside to Jesus.

- Pressed in by people
on every side, someone
finally said to him:

"*All of your brothers and mother*
*are waiting outside for you,*
*wanting to speak with you there.*"

Then Jesus looked round
at all gathered here, saying:

"*Who is my **mother** though?*
*Who are my **brothers** then?*"

Pointing toward his disciples, he added:

"*Here, all around me,*
*my mother and brothers*
*are sitting with me!*
*For whoever fulfilleth the will*
*of my Father in Heaven is*
*brother or sister or mother to me!*"

(M 3:31-34 / Mt 12:46-50 / L 8:19-21)

## 85. IN ALL ISRAEL KNOWN

JESUS TOURED ALL OVER GALILEE,
teaching inside of its temples,
announcing *GOOD NEWS*
of God's Kingdom
continually
curing their illnesses,
washing away all disease. —

News of his wonders spread wide,
all through Syria;
those who
were brought
to him suffered
afflictions of every kind:

those in hells of pain or
cursed with demons, and
those having seizures, and
those who could not move
around - *Jesus cured them all.*

*- those in hells of pain or cursed with demons, and those having seizures, and those who could not move around -* **Jesus cured them all**

Massive crowds
came here from
Galilee and from
Decapolis, Judea,
also Jerusalem, and
    from the regions
encircling the Jordan.

*And all of them*
        *followed*
                *him round.*

(Mt 4:23-25)

## VI. <u>**HEALING**</u>

*Heal me Lord and*
***I shall be*** HEALED —

*Save me and **I shall be***
SAVED —
        *YOU are*
*the one I praise.*

JEREMIAH 17:14

## 86. THE FAITH OF A ROMAN

AFTER JESUS WAS DONE
with his preaching there,
he travelled onward still.

Back in Capernaum
there came
a centurion to him,
requesting
his urgent help. —

The centurion's servant,
by master **so *treasured***,
was close to the grave
for death breathed near.

Jesus's name had been told
this commander,
who sent Jewish elders
to fetch him, to heal his servant now.

When the elders arrived before Jesus,
they begged him in earnest tones:

"This Roman deserves
your assistance —
he values our nation,
constructed **our temple**
             for us."

Hearing this, Jesus
went right along
with them. —

As soon as he got there,
this Roman said:

"*Lord, my servant
so loyal was hit with
paralysis — he is in
         terrible pain.*"

To which Jesus replied:

"*Ought I come there
and heal him?*"

The centurion said: "*O
my Lord, I'm not worthy
of you in my house;*

*I am not even worthy
to seek you out here but*
**just** *say the word* then
  my servant is cured.

*For I know what it means
to command with authority
troops who are under my word.*

*— For to one I say* **'Go'**,
*and he goes on his way,
then another tell* **'Come'**,
*and he comes to me then.*

*Like I say to my
    servant 'Do this'
        or 'Do that' and
            he does it for me."*

Every word that he heard
  more amazed Jesus was,
    then to crowds who
      were following
        him, **he said**:

*"To all of you here
in this land I say
I have not found
EVEN ONE **Israelite**
who has has shown me
such faith as I see in **this man**.*

*I tell you that
multitudes East
and West will come
gathering here — find
their place at the FEAST
beside Abraham, Isaac and
Jacob in HEAVEN'S KINGDOM.*

*Even subjects of that place
shall even be exiled and
hurled into darkness,
and **there** shall be
wailing and
grinding of teeth."*

Then he told
the centurion:

"*Go, **IT IS SO**, as
thy faith believes it.*"

*At **that** very instant —*
his servant was healed.

After that,
all went back
to the house and
they found that
the servant
         *was totally cured.*


(Mt 8:5-13 / L 7:1-10 )

## 87. FROM DEATH TO LIFE

IMMEDIATELY AFTER THIS
Jesus went on to
a town
called *Nain*
and his followers,
large crowds, came along too.

As he came to the town gate
a cadaver was being
carried on out —
sole son of his mother,
        a widow besides.

A great mass of people were
gathered around her -
when Lord Jesus
saw her,
his heart,
it cried also
while to her he said:

    "*Do not cry* — ***cry not.***"

Jesus went to the stretcher
upon which the body was
carried and touched it —
the bearer stopped still,
and then Jesus spoke out:

"— *Young man, I tell you,*
**Get up from there now!**"

The dead man sat upright
and started to speak and
    **thus** Jesus returned
to the mother her son. -

Everyone standing there
gasped in awe and their
    GOD they praised:

"*A prophet so mighty*
*appeareth among us.*
*Now* GOD *has come down*
*to anoint his people!*"

The news about Jesus spread far and wide,
reaching all through Judea to *everywhere*.


(L 7:11-17)

## 88. THE PRICE OF FAITH

WHEN JESUS SAW
all of the crowds who
surrounded him,
he ordered them
to the lake's far side.

It was then
that a tutor in Law
came to him and said:

*"Teacher, O Rabbi, I want
to come with you,*
**WHEREVER**
**YOU GO."**

To which
Jesus responded:

*"The foxes have dens and
the birds have their nests
yet the* SON OF MAN
*nowhere to
rest his head."*

A different disciple
was saying to Jesus:

"*Lord, I must first go
and bury my father*",

but Jesus said,

"— *DO NOT DO SO,
just follow me now
for **the dead** are
the ones who must
bury **the dead**.*"


(Mt 8:18-22)

# 89. "EVEN THE WINDS AND WAVES"

AS DAY TURNED TO EVENING
Jesus proposed: *"To yonder, far
    shore of the lake let us go."*

- Leaving the masses of people
behind them,
they took Jesus aboard the boat,
his disciples
set out after them, other boats
                  alongside.

While they sailed across,
Jesus fell deep in sleep and
a wind of sheer violence cut
straight through the sea —
swirling tempest of rage,
the waves crashed over
them and the boat was
near sunk - with deep
waters full swamped

*- every life at risk -*

> "Ye people of **such slender faith!**
> Where has gone your belief?
> **Why are you so afraid?**"

- Yet all the while
Jesus was sleeping
right up at the stern
on a mattress when
        suddenly,
      he was awoken,
     disciples cried out
      to him, shouting:

"*Rabbi,*
***don't you even care***
***if we drown?***
*O please save us,*
*Lord Jesus,*
***or we will be drowned!***"

Jesus woke and exclaimed
       to his followers:

"*What is this?*
    *Ye people*
*of **such slender faith**!*
*Where has gone your*
*belief?* ***Why are you***
***so afraid?*** — "

Then he got to his feet
and
with words he rebuked
both
the winds and the waves
saying:
"SILENCE, BE CALM!" —

The winds
stopped blowing,
the lake became still.

They were shaken with
terror and awe,
and asked: "**What kind of man is this?**
*Even the winds and the waves they obey him*
**his every command!**"

(M 4:35-41 / Mt 8:23-27 / L 8:22-25)

## 90. "DEMONS BEGONE!"

ACROSS THE LAKE
from Galilee
they sailed to
Gadara's coast

- they moored
their craft then
Jesus set his feet
upon the shore.

The instant that
he did so, there
came forth a man
of soul impure —

who, catching sight
of Jesus, ran to see
Him - naked
to his knees
did fall,
*cried*
*out:*

*"What
do you
want of us
- Jesus - **Son
of God on High**?*

Possessed by
demons, many
years, he wore
no clothes at all,

no longer lived
in human house
- the tombs his
home become.

Before, he had
been chained in
irons - none could
bind him any more;

he broke all bonds
of hand and foot,
tore up his chains,
no man could tame.

His wails and cries
the lonely hills
would echo
day and night;

he cut his skin with
stones all over -
*violent* - no-one
passed this way.

As loud as lungs
could shout,
again he shouted:

"*What*
*do you*
*want of us*
*- Jesus - Son*
*of God on High?*"

And then
Jesus
answered:

"*OUT, BEGONE,*
*THOU UNCLEAN SPIRIT -*
*LEAVE THIS POOR MAN'S*
*SOUL I SAY!*"

Yet as Jesus exhorted
the demons
depart,
they yelled
at Him loud, they cried:

"*Why come you here*
*to **torture us** WHILE*
*IT IS NOT YET TIME?*"

So Jesus asked him:

"*Tell me then,*
*what is **thy name**?*"

To which he answered:

"***Legion**,*
*for many am I!*"

And *this could*
*be believed* - for
the spirits took over
with power supreme -

all shackles they shattered
all manacles mangled,
no guards could
hold them down.

This multitude
of demons
begged:

"*Have mercy,*
*we pray, do not*
*banish us 'NOWHERE'!*

**Hurl us not into**

**the gaping**

**Abyss!**"

Upon the hill
beside them, pigs
were feeding there
in massive herds,

    - the demons
entreated of Jesus:

"*Let us now go into
these unholy hogs!*"

They pleaded and
pleaded for Jesus
to send them:

"*Drive us out
into these pigs
— **nowhere else!**"*

    - Jesus
granted this
with *just a **single**
command*:

"*DEMONS **BEGONE!***"

And the spirits unclean,
to the swine they fled

— At that instant
the herd,
two thousand vast,
they
stampeded, charged
downhill
the lake's steep bank

to the edge of the cliff

they raced and

*LEAPT*

off the edge they

plunged into the waters

- then drowned

and died

— **every**

**single one**

All those
who tended
the swine *ran off
fast* in a state of fear

- Those
who saw
what had
happened
spread word
far and wide;
in town and in
country this tale
they described:

*of a man cured
of demons,
of pigs that had
perished -*
**the witnesses'
stories
brought people
in droves -**

*for they had to see
Jesus and
what he had done.*

BUT IN SEEING IT

ALL IN SHEER

TERROR

FROZE

UP

*Sane
there he sat*
they discovered,
the man plagued by
demons before -
NOW ALL
GONE

Free of
the *legion*,
he sat there
by Jesus' feet -
dressed and calm.

*The Gadarenes
all in dread
stopped
dead.*

Those
who witnessed
what happened
told
those
who arrived of
what Jesus had
done

*- how the raving
demoniac now
was at peace
and **cured**.*

After that
all the people
came up to Jesus -

beseeching him **leave**:

"*PART OUR LAND*

*RETURN NOT!*"

— So immediately
Jesus departed,
the vessel
rejoining
- yet just
as he stepped
on the boat, then
the exorcised one came
along and implored of him:

"*Master! -*
*Let me go with you! -*
*MASTER, LET ME COME WITH YOU!*"

But
Jesus replied:

"*No!*
**Go back**
*to your home -*

*to the people you
know - and tell them
of* WHAT GOD HAS
DONE FOR YOU*! -*

**Let them know
with what mercies
thou hast been
blessed!"**

So
when Jesus departed
the man
went to all of Decapolis
telling how
demons were cast out
from
him *by his Master*

AND

ALL OF

THE PEOPLE

WERE STUNNED.

(M 5:1-31 / Mt 8:28-34 / L 8:26-39)

## 91. SICKNESS UNTO DEATH

JESUS SAILED AGAIN
to the lake's farther side
and returned to his home
        in Capernaum.
After so many healings,
awaited and welcomed,
he sets foot on shore, then
the masses crowd round him.

He teaches the lesson of
owine in its wineskins —
a synagogue leader comes over
to Jesus — *Jairus* by name.

The instant he set eyes on
Jesus, he fell to his knees
at His feet and implored:

*"My daughter, my only one
- now only twelve - she is ill
now and **dying**. - Come out to
my house, lay your hands on her
        — **then she will live!"***

Jesus rose and advanced,
his disciples came after him,
    following Jairus, with
  multitudes following,
crushing them in.

There, 'mid the masses,
was one who for
twelve long years suffered
great bleedings,
and gave to the doctors all
money she had —
yet her state only worsened.

On hearing of *Jesus*, she came
up behind him and reached
out to touch just the edge
of his robe, thinking:

*"If I can only touch*
*part of his garment,*
*then I will be healed."*

Her bleeding, it stopped,
she was **free of all pain**.

Jesus felt, at that moment,
the power drawn out of him,
turned to the crowd and asked:
*"Who touched my robe?"*

Every person **denied** doing this
and then Peter said,
*"Master, the people are pressing from
every side, yet still
you ask of them, 'Who touched me?'"*

Yet still Jesus insisted: *"No,
someone has touched me,
I sense it - for power has
drained fully out of me."*

Jesus looked round him
to see who had done this.
The woman knew just what
had happened to her,

— she could hide no more,
stepped out and fell at his feet,
she was trembling with fear
and to him *confessed all*.

Before all the people
the woman explained
why she touched him and
how she was instantly cured.

Knelt there before him,
he said to her: *"Take heart,*
*my daughter, thy strong faith*
*has healed thee — now go off*
*in peace and **be free of thy pain**."*


Just as Jesus was saying this,
people came out of the house
of Jairus - speaking dark words:

*"Thy daughter is **already dead**,"*
they said — *"there's no need*
*to bother the rabbi now!"*

Hearing this, Jesus told Jairus:

*"**Be thou not afraid**,*
   *you must only BELIEVE,*
     ***then she** WILL BE SAVED."*

Jesus, he would not let anyone follow,
just Peter and James - with
his brother John.

As they came near the house
they saw chaos,
commotion, *so many*
were weeping and wailing loud.

— Jesus entered the building
and hearing those playing
their dirges on pipes,
he said: "***Go from***
***here now!*** *Stop*
*this mayhem and mourning!*
*The girl, she is sleeping,* ***not dead!***"

But those standing there
laughed at this, mocking him,
    *certain* that she was dead.

After all gathered here
had been sent on their way,
Jesus and his disciples were shown
by the parents where their daughter lay.

*Jesus went in her room,
reaching out to her,
taking her by the hand
as he says:* **"Get up, my child!"**

Jesus went in her room,
reaching out to her,
taking her by
the hand
as he says:

*"Get up, my child!"*

Her spirit returned
to her all at once, she got
up to her feet, walked around!

At this,
all there were totally awestruck
but Jesus
gave orders *to let no-one know
of this —*
**everything that had occurred.**

- Then he told them
to give her some food.

        *News of this miracle
        spread far and wide.*

(M 5:21-43 / Mt 9:1; 9:18-26 / L 8:40-56)

# 92. ALL ADVERSITIES ARE OVERCOME

AS JESUS PROCEEDED
two blind men walked
after him, calling out:
"*Mercy, o mercy, have mercy
 upon us, o David's son!*"

Even once Jesus had gone inside,
they still followed on after
him, so he asked:

"*Do ye both believe
truly that I can
heal you?*"

And they answered:

"**Yes Lord, o yes, o yes!**"

So Jesus put his fingers
onto their eyes and
he said: "*In accord
 with your faith,
 **may ye both be cured.**"

At once, as their sight was restored to them, Jesus said sternly: "*You must see that no-one else learns of this.*"

But when they left,
then they spoke widely of
what he had done for them,
     all through the region.

Just as Jesus departed there one was brought out who was demon-possessed and *who could not talk.*

After Jesus had cast out
the evil spirits, —
then he who *was* mute,
**he could speak once again.**

The many around who were witnessing this were astonished and people were saying:

*"Never before have
such things in all Israel
**ever been seen.**"*

Yet the Pharisees
   still said:

*"'Tis only through Beelzebub
 - prince of all demons -
  that Jesus is able
   to chase them out."*


(Mt 9:27-34)

# 93. "ARE YOU THE ONE?"

DISCIPLES OF JOHN
came to see him
in prison,
recounting him
all of the things that occurred.

After hearing the deeds
of 'MESSIAH', he summoned
two followers, Jesus to ask:

> "Are you **the one**
> who was spoken of? —
> Do we await someone else?"

When the men came
to Jesus, they asked
what John wanted:

> "The Baptist has sent
> us to come here and find
> out — are you who was
> spoken of **or do we wait
> for** ANOTHER **besides?**' "

In that period, Jesus
was curing *so many* —
diseases and maladies,
people possessed by dark
spirits and those who were
blind - *given sight back again.*

Jesus answered the messengers:

"*Go back to John now,
report to him all that
you* **see** *and* **hear** *— that
the blind become sighted,
the crippled can walk, that
the lepers are cleansed and
the deaf hear once more.*

*Tell how* **dead** *are raised
up to new* LIFE *and Good News
is revealed* **to the poor**.
*Blessèd be all those who do not*
       *fall*
      *down*
  *or falter*
        **because**
        **of me**."

At the moment John's followers
started to leave,
Jesus set
about telling
the crowds of him:

>"*Have you been
to the wilderness? -
What have you seen?
- A reed that was swayed
by the wind? — If not that,
then WHAT WERE YOU **expecting
to** SEE?    Did you go
out to see a gent dressed in
rich robes? - No, for those
who wear fine garments
wallow in luxuries, live
in GRAND PALACES
fit for KINGS.*
>
> *So tell me again, WHO you went
out to see? — A prophet?*
> **O yes, but not just
any prophet.**

HE is the one **of whom
it has been writ**:

' - Ahead of you
I send my HERALD
who shall pave the way
                for **you**'.

    Forsooth, I say to you,
   no man of woman born
was ever greater than
the Baptist — **yet still,**

who is even the slightest
in HEAVEN's KINGDOM
is **greater** than **he**!

From time of John
unto this very day,
the KINGDOM has been
    languishing in
      throes of **violence**
        — **violent ones**
        have made their
           raids upon it.

*All of the Law*
*and the Prophets*
*have told what came*
*before the time of John.*

*And if all you who* **hear**
**me** *are willed to accept it,*
    *in truth is the Baptist*
    Elijah *returned whom*
    *we waited for long —*
    whosoever has ears,
**let them hear this from me!"**

The populace - even collectors
of taxes - on hearing
these words, agreed
Jesus was right,
*for* **they had been**
**baptized** *by* John *himself.*

    Yet the Pharisees, teachers
of Law, and the rest, they rejected
God's purpose was true of themselves.

*They had not been baptized by John.*

Jesus carried on speaking:

"*With whom*
*to compare this new generation?*
*Like children they seem, those who*
*sit in the marketplace — calling*
*out loud to those passing by:*

'*We played on the pipes for you*
*yet ye danced not;*
*sang psalms of the dead yet*
*ye would not mourn*'.

*The Baptist, you see,*
*he came fasting - not eating*
*of bread and nor drinking of wine -*
*yet they said, 'He has devils inside of him'.*

*But now, when the* S*on of* M*an*
*cometh, both* **eating and drinking**,
*instead they say:*

"*Here is a glutton -*
*a glutton and drunkard*
*- companion to sinners,*
*collectors of taxes'.*

*However,*

   *WISDOM,*

      *you shall see,*

         *is proven true*

      *by actions —*

*her own offspring."*


(Mt 11:2-19 / L 7:18-35)

## 94. ANOINTED WITH TEARS

WHEN A PHARISEE ASKED
Jesus over to dine,
he went into
their home,
at their table reclined.

A woman from that town,
of sinful life,
learned that Jesus was visiting
this man's house,
so she up turned that day with
fragranced ointment
              in alabaster jar.

While she stood behind Jesus
and wept at his feet,
she had started to moisten
them with her tears.

She wiped them and wet them
with her own hair, and
then kissed his feet,
pouring her perfume all over.

When the man who invited him
saw what was happening, inside
his mind he was thinking this:

*"If this man here were truly*
*a prophet then he would know*
*she who is touching him reeks of*
*sin, and what type of a woman*
*she really is."*

Hearing his innermost thoughts,
Jesus answered him, saying:

*"Dear Simon, to you I have*
*something to say…"*

*"Tell me, o rabbi"*, he said.

*"Picture a lender of money*
*whom two people owe.*

*One owes five hundred denarii,*
*— the other one owes fifty alone.*

<u>*Neither of them*</u> *could repay him*
*and so* **he forgave them their debts**.

*Tell me now, what you think of this -*
*which of his debtors will*
                *love him the more?"*

To this, Simon said quickly:

"*I'm thinking, the one of whose*
       *debts was the largest.*"

"*I think that you judge*
  *things correctly*", said Jesus.

He turned to the woman,
to Simon he said:
                "*Now **look at**
**this woman** — I came in your house
and you gave me no water to cleanse
my feet, yet she bathed my feet with
her tears and she wiped them dry
with her hair. You did not think
to kiss me yet this one, as soon
as I entered, has kissed my feet
**ceaselessly**. While you gave
no oil to put on my head,
she anoints my feet with
an unction supreme.*

*Therefore — I say to you —*
**her sins** *have been* EXPUNGED *as*
*the depth of her Love here has shown.*

*Yet the one who has only*
*been pardoned for little things,*
*their love will clearly be* **less than**
                                 **the other.**"

Jesus turned to her, saying then:

"*Thy sins have all been forgiven.*"

The guests dining with them,
between themselves spoke thus:

"**Who is this man** that
                 *he can forgive sins?*"

     — After all else,
Jesus said to the woman:
               "*Thy faith has*
*redeemed thee – now go in* PEACE."


(L 7:36-50)

## 95. HEALERS FOR THE KINGDOM

TRAVELING ALL AROUND
the region,
through towns and villages,
preaching
in synagogues, Jesus proclaimed
G*ood* N*ews*
of the Kingdom while healing
infirmities
           everywhere.

As he looked on the crowds,
he felt
only compassion, for they were
so haggard
and helpless and hopeless — like
sheep who have
got no shepherd to guard them.

He spoke to his followers:

*"See here, the harvest,*
*so plentiful, yet just how*
*few are the harvesters.*

*Let us ask then*

*the Lord of the Harvest*

*to send out*
        *more harvesters*
*into his fields*
        *to harvest."*


(Mt 9:35-38)

## 96. **HEALING UPON A DAY OF REST**

SOME TIME AFTER THAT
Jesus went to Jerusalem,
marking a Jewish feast.

Now there was in that city
a pool near the *Sheep Gate*,
'Bethesda', in dialect
it has been called —
a fine place protected
by five rows of columns.

In that setting, numberless
invalids used to lie down and
to rest: the blind and the lame
and the crippled, and more. -

A man who was there at this time
had been suffering
thirty-eight years.
- Jesus found him
lain there, learnt
      how long it had been.

He asked:

"*Do you **not want***
   *to get well, after all?*"

"*Dear sir*", said the ailing one,
"*there is nobody to help me*
   *here — into this pool —*
   *once it has been stirred.*

*Each time that I try*
*to get in, other people*
*just push right in*
              *front of me.*"

After that, Jesus said:
"**Stand up now** *— pick*
*up thy mat and WALK!*"

And instantly then did
the invalid pick up his mat
and **walk**. He was healed *at once*.

- The day upon which this
took place was a Sabbath,
some synagogue leaders,
accused the one cured:

"*You break the law, for today is
the Sabbath - **you carry your mat**!*"

But he answered: "*The man who
has cured me, he said to me:
'**Pick up thy mat and walk!**'*"

Then they asked him: "*So WHO is
this man who has bid you to do this
- to pick up your mat and walk?*"

The man who was cured had no
inkling who Jesus was — he who had
now slipped away in the crowds.

Later on, Jesus found him again
at the temple and told him:

"*You see, now you're well! So **sin
no more** — YOU MAY BEFALL WORSE.*"

The man left and he let Jewish elders
know *Jesus*
was he who had made him well.

(J 5:1-15)

## 97. "WHAT THE FATHER DOES, THE SON DOES ALSO"

AS JESUS ACCOMPLISHED
these acts on a Sabbath,
the synagogue leaders
began to harass him.

Defending himself,
Jesus told them:

*"My Father works
constantly — each,
every day — and thus
also I am working
constantly too."*

After this, they had
even more hunger to kill him,
for not only did he
break laws of the Sabbath but
claimed that his
personal Father **was GOD!** - thus
**is crowning
himself** as an EQUAL with **GOD!**

Jesus provided this answer to them:

> "*So verily, I say to ye,*
> *by himself the S*ON *can*
> *accomplish nothing —*
> *all he can do is to imitate*
> *that which he sees his Father do.*
>
> *For what the Father does,*
> *the son does also.*
> *— You see, as*
> *the Father loves the son,*
> **He shows him all that He can do***.*
>
> *Indeed, He shall show his S*ON
> **feats far greater***,*
> *in order that* YOU *may gaze on*
>                        **in amazement***.*
>
> *The same way the Father makes*
> **dead** RESURRECT, *gives their life*
> *back to them — so the S*ON *also*
> *breathes back the life into those*
> **with whom** HE **is well pleased***.*

*— Beyond that, the FATHER,
HE judges no-one,
puts trust in
His SON to be **Judge of All** -*

*so that all may honor the Son
as they honor the Father
who **sent** HIM **down here**.*

*Those who do not show honor
to Son, they dishonor
the Father who sent him too.*

*In all truth do I say to you,
you who are listening, you
who believe in the ONE
who sent me - you shall
possess the Life Eternal
— YOU SHALL NOT BE
JUDGED: you have crossed
the bridge from **Death** to LIFE.*

*O so **truly** I tell you there cometh
a time when the **dead** shall hear
speaking the voice of GOD's SON
— and **who hear**, SHALL LIVE.*

*For just as the Father harbors* LIFE
*in Himself, thus He grants*
*His Son also to*
*hold* LIFE *within him,*
 *and* POWER TO JUDGE
  HE *has given Him also,*
   *as He is the* SON *of* MAN.

*I say to you, be not astounded at this,*
*for the time cometh soon*
*those* **who sleep in their graves**
*shall hear* HIS *voice — and* ARISE.
 *those whose actions were good*
  *will rise up and* **live**; *those*
  *whose actions were evil*
   *will rise to eternal*
   **condemnation.**

*- On my own, there is nothing that*
*I can accomplish.*
*I judge only things as I hear of them.*
*I judge things fairly.*
*I do not desire to please my own self,*
   **only** HE **who sent me**.*"*

(J 5:16-30)

**BOOK** of **JESUS**

# THE TASK IS THE TESTIMONY

"*NOW IF **I** MAKE STATEMENTS*
*about mine **own self**,*
*then that which*
*I testify IS NOT TRUE,*

*but if someone else testifies*
*in my favor —*
*I know what*
*they testify: IT IS THE TRUTH.*

*You sent the Baptist testifying*
*what **is** TRUE, but do*
*not suppose*
*to yourself that*
*I place trust in human witness*

*— I mention this only in case*
　　　*it may lead you*
*towards SALVATION.*

*John was a lamp whose flame*
*burned bright;*
*you selected **a time***
*would be blessed by his light.*

*But the body of evidence*
*I present you*
*is more powerful*
*even than that of John.*

*— For what I enact,*
***this** the FATHER has asked*
*me to bring to COMPLETION —*
***each thing** I do now proves*
*that it was the LORD UP*
*ABOVE who sent me.*

*And even the Father*
*who sends me, HE testifies*
*all that I do - though **you hear***
***not** HIS VOICE **nor perceive** HIS FORM.*

*The WORD does not LIVE WITHIN YOU*
***because you believe not** in*
*the one whom HE sent.*

*You sit at your* SCRIPTURES *and*
*study them carefully,*
*thinking in them*
*to find* LIFE ETERNAL.

*Exactly* THOSE WRITINGS
*are testament*
**to me** –
*yet still you*
*turn down the* LIFE  **I offer you**.

*From humans*
*I take in no glory* –
*yet it is* TRUE: **I do know you**.

*I know that in your hearts*
GOD's LOVE **does not live**

*In His name I have come*
*but* **you do not embrace me**

*— yet somebody else comes*
*to you* **in their own name**,
*you welcome them openly.*

*How can ye even BELIEVE?*
*— for ye revel in glory*
*you give to each other*
*yet search not for glory*
*that comes from ONE GOD ALONE.*

*However, think not that*
*when I am in front of my Father*
*- and speaking of you -*
*that I shall* **make accusations***.*

*— The one who accuses you,*
***it is not I*** *but MOSES on whom*
*all your hopes have long hinged.*

*If you really believed in HIM*
*then you would also*
*believe in ME TOO*
*for he wrote words ABOUT ME.*

*But if you believe not the words*
*that were writ then what chance is*
*there you will BELIEVE WHAT **I SAY**?"*

(J 5:31-47)

"— *For what I enact,* **this** *the Father has asked me to bring to* COMPLETION"

## THE END

OF

## VOLUME I

## BOOK of JESUS

A UNIFIED GOSPEL
IN ENGLISH VERSE

## — *Apologia Poetæ* —
### THE POET'S APOLOGY

*by* Edouard d'Araille

THE IDEA OF COMPOSING a 'gospel harmony' in English verse was one that was initially proposed to me about five years ago, in 2020. At that time it was a raw concept, though the core idea, which was to make the poetic chapters *as close as possible* to the source texts (the four canonical gospels) was already there. The magnitude of challenge this task would prove to be was not something that was appreciated at the outset.

However, over the first year of developing this work, the format, style and approach would start to take shape. It became clear that the poetic text would be divided into chapters, each one focused on a specific incident in Jesus's life, whether this was based on one or more of the evangelists' accounts. With the composition of the very first chapter in 2021 - the section of the current volume called *"Demons Begone!"* - a flexible form of writing style would begin to emerge. No specific meter or rhyming style was chosen for the volume as a whole, instead the style of poetry was allowed to be individualized to every single chapter. This was not to be a gospel composed in sonnets, or something else artificially constraining like that. As for approach, it became one that was driven by faithfulness to the source texts and to research-based reasoning into all aspects of them, above all as historical evidence.

For those readers who are unfamiliar with this particular literary form, a 'gospel harmony' is an attempt at bringing the content of the four gospels together in a single work, so that the reader may appreciate the narrative of the gospels in a more unified way than by reading them separately. However, some of the most difficult challenges to face, apart from the fact that the accounts of a specific event can sometimes differ a lot between the gospels, are the issues of *chronology*.

Although there is a general agreement on the overall order of the gospel incidents, there are at the same time many issues of dispute about the actual sequence of events in Jesus's life. This is especially obvious in one type of 'harmony', in which the passages from the four gospels are set alongside each other in columns so that it can be seen how they agree and how they differ. Such a text is called 'synoptic' as the relationship between the separate accounts can easily be seen at one glance (*'syn'* = with; *'optic'* = eye/s — "with one eye"). By viewing the passages in this way, it can be seen, for example, that the incident of Jesus becoming enraged at the synagogue being treated like a marketplace and throwing everyone out, finds itself in a different stage of the account in John (where it appears near the beginning of his gospel) than in the synoptic gospels - of Matthew, Mark and Luke - where the incident occurs near the end instead. Another example is that of Jesus being anointed with a perfumed ointment while at a dinner, which occurs in all four gospels. However, while in Matthew, Mark and John the incident happens just in advance of Jesus's death, in Luke it happens during the middle of his ministry.

In the latter case, the confusion is even greater as the accounts also differ in terms of where the incident took place and who was present, which makes it hard to determine if the accounts are based on the same event in all cases, or whether they are recounting more than one event. In fact, in both of the two examples just referred to, it is possible (though not proveable) that Jesus not only flew into a rage in one temple, on one occasion, but that this happened more than once and that it is *plausible* that John represented a different incident from the other evangelists. As locations at which the anointing of Jesus with a perfumed unction - as well as the persons mentioned as being present - also vary significantly, it can be speculated that the New Testament gospel accounts may be referring to more than one occasion on which this happened.

In composing this new verse translation of the gospels, which combines them into one harmonized narrative, tough choices must sometimes be made, without knowing if those choices are correct or misguided. For example, regarding the above incidents — where and when they took place, whether they occurred once or more, who exactly was involved *etc*. To give another example which is relevant to volume one of 'Book of Jesus', in the section devoted to casting out demons and sending them into a herd of pigs who run off the edge of a cliff at Jesus's command (S.90), while in Mark's and Luke's gospels there is **one** possessed man who is healed by Jesus, in the gospel of Matthew, he writes of two persons possessed, though from all the other details provided it is unquestionably the same event that is being reported — *what choice to make?*

Sometimes, decisions have been made in favor of the version of events that is portrayed in *more* of the source texts — for example, in this case, as two gospels depict only one possessed man, while the third one depicts two, the choice has been made that there is only one demon-possessed man. Although one overriding objective has been to synthesize one integrated narrative from four distinct gospel accounts, which often means that multiple reports of an event are being fused into a single episode, which generally enriches the level of detail, the problem is that it is often in the smaller details that there are minor differences between the four evangelists, so there are usually many minor choices to make when composing chapters that combine accounts from more than one gospel. In fact, it would be fair to say that on every other page of this book (half of them, that is) decisions had to be made in favor of the details of one or other version, the choices being harder when the degree of difference is greater, and easier when the discrepancy between versions is of a less pronounced nature.

In contrast with those gospel harmonies that provide an at-a-glance overview of how the gospel texts vary - setting the various versions of an incident alongside each other in columns - this work presents an attempt at synthesizing the accounts into one narrative, in spite of the conflicting details and differences of chronology, location and persons involved. Though this type of harmony is more likely to lead to a final text that openly varies from details presented in one or more gospel accounts, I believe that what is gained in enabling the reader to follow one, unified account, is greater than any loss.

Since the first known gospel harmony, written around 160 A.D. by Tatian, up to the present day, there have been many attempts at presenting the texts of the gospel in a way that either shows their detailed inter-relationships or combine their incidents and teachings into one continuous narrative. Though it was written before a century of many developments in Bible scholarship, '*A Translation Harmony and Analysis of the Gospels*' (1892) by Leo Tolstoy is one of the most impressive attempts at doing so by an acclaimed literary author. In fact, though Tolstoy has based his work on the original Koine Greek gospels, the level of his writing skills raises his version of them to the height of being a classic of literature at the same time as being a Bible translation. For the most part, however, gospel harmonies have been assembled or composed by religious scholars and not by recognized authors. A writer of Tolstoy's stature producing a gospel harmony, is a rare exception.

Tatian's 2nd Century 'Diatessaron' appears to be the first work to have unified the four gospels into a unified account. By doing so, it reduced the work by around a thousand verses, by not including duplicate versions of episodes or teachings. The reality is that Tatian's harmony became an accepted lectionary gospel text in a number of Syriac-speaking churches, for around four centuries. For the most part, though, the individual gospels have been given priority while harmonies have been of secondary importance. Here, however, is not the place to conduct a review of gospel harmonies; their number is vast, their history long — the present afterword is only intended to share a few reflections on the current work's composition.

Perhaps the most challenging aspect of a work like the present - of any unified gospel harmony in fact - is that each of the evangelists had different backgrounds, purposes and audiences, such that in creating a single gospel from all four, the individuality of the original writers and their gospels is inevitably lost, while at the same time it is hoped that other, positive gains may be made through the process of uniting them.

Although, in the early days of the church, the Gospel of Matthew was considered to be the first (in order of writing) of the gospels, the established consensus is currently that the Gospel of Mark was composed first, by a companion of St. Peter called Mark, one of Jesus's original disciples - reputedly the founder of the Church of Alexandria. That gospel was written for an audience of gentiles (non-Jews) probably in Rome, and particularly presents Jesus as a "suffering servant" of God, though during most of the gospel he is presented as not wishing for it to be known that he is the Messiah predicted in the Old Testament. He wants it to be kept a secret. It is estimated to have been written in approximately 70 ACE.

The gospel that is presented as the first one, in the *order* of the New Testament, is that of Matthew, and though it was for a long time deemed to have been written by the apostle of that name, this is now considered to be both problematic and unlikely. Noteworthy to mention about this gospel, is that it wanted to emphasize the importance of preserving the original Jewish traditions, which its author appeared to fear were being lost in a church which was growing larger with a gentile audience - thus the audience of Matthew can be considered to be Jews as much as non-Jews. It is generally agreed as having been written in the last quarter of the 1st Century ACE. The majority of scholars believe that it relies on an additional source called '**Q**' (for 'Quelle', German for *source*), a 'sayings gospel' - a collection of teachings rather than a biographical account.

The third gospel appearing in the New Testament is the Gospel of Luke. It is possible that its author was a companion of St. Paul, but as with the other gospels, its writer is anonymous. What we do know, is that its author is also responsible for the book entitled 'Acts of the Apostles', which documents how the Twelve Apostles spread the gospel after Jesus was no longer with them on Earth. Almost 30% of the New Testament is by the evangelist we call Luke. He is believed to have been a physician and a companion of Paul, the apostle, while as author of a gospel and 'Acts', he functions as an historian. It is worth noting that he is the main gospel author to refer to Jesus as '*Savior*'. The text of his gospel combines what is found in Mark with the source '**Q**' that Matthew also relied upon, as well as a source named 'L' — material *unique* to his gospel. It is usually viewed as having been written between 80-90 ACE.

Finally, in order of appearance in the New Testament, and last of the canonical gospels, is the Gospel of John. Like the other gospels, its author is unknown although it is believed that its content derived from the "disciple whom Jesus loved" — a phrase which appears half a dozen times in that gospel. It is dated between 90-110 ACE, though it appears to have originated as early as 70 ACE. It is clearly distinguished from the three other gospels because, whereas *Mark*, *Matthew* and *Luke* share a body of material with each other and have many similarities due to that, the Gospel of John does not derive from any of the same sources, though there is nonetheless remarkable agreement between the synoptic gospels and that of *John*, giving further historical confirmation of Jesus. This gospel and three epistles attributed to him, as well as the 'Book of Revelation', are viewed as one body of work, referred to as 'Johannine', yet few consider them the work of a single author.

The '*Book of Jesus*', presented here in three volumes (of which this is the first) as a 'Unified Gospel in English Verse', is based on the entire text of the four canonical gospels described above. However, while considering the order of events and especially the order of Jesus's teachings, reference has also been made to the body of almost fifty apocryphal gospels that appeared over the first few centuries after Jesus's life. There are issues with the 'authority' of all them, yet it is the opinion of the current translator that even though they furnish no additional, reliable episodes that could be included in Jesus's biography, it is helpful to be aware of the wider tradition of writings about Jesus. The 'Gospel of Thomas', for example, is a prime example of a 'sayings gospel', a collection of wisdom taught by Jesus and circulating in the times soon after Jesus's life on Earth. Considered by some scholars to date from as early as 60 ACE, earlier even than the Gospel of Mark, but this is not yet sufficiently corroborated. It is especially interesting as it appears to be similar to the kind of sayings gospel that is a common source of the synoptic gospels, called source 'Q', giving us some insight into what that kind of "proto-gospel" may have looked like. However, as iterated before, the text of this new poetic translation is **only** textually based on the four canon gospels and *no material from any others is included.*

The question of whether an earlier gospel existed, written in Hebrew or Aramaic, is one that has not yet been answered. It is known as the 'Hebrew Gospel Hypothesis' and was initiated in the 2nd Century ACE when a bishop named Papias of Hierapolis went on record as saying that the *original gospel* was written by Matthew the Apostle, and that this work was in Hebrew. The theory was that the Gospel of Matthew (as we know it) was a translation into Koine Greek of that earlier Jewish gospel. This novel theory was also maintained by St. Jerome and survived in some form or another to this day; however, the general academic consensus is that the theory is untenable — unless future excavations prove otherwise.

The way in which this work has been composed was in three key phases. *Initially*, each of the gospels was individually translated into verse, with reference to the original Greek and consideration of all the prose translations that have been published to date (of which almost fifty merit attention). *Secondly*, in those cases where two, three or all four gospels provided an account of the same episode or teaching, the different poetized versions of the gospel passages were combined into a single text, being careful not to add anything that was not in the gospel and cautious not to miss anything out either.

This was, in some way, the most demanding stage, as it was vital not to ignore the richness of details provided by the varying accounts, while at the same time many challenges had to be faced in terms of elements in the accounts that seemed, on the surface of things, to be in conflict with each other. *Thirdly,* after a versified form of each section of the overall narrative was arrived at, further research was conducted so as to make sure that the final poetic chapters would pay attention to the results of modern scriptural scholarship. As there is disagreement of various kinds in regard to almost every passage in the gospels, it was a matter of arriving at a final form of all translated passages that would strike a compromise between many differing points of view. Though the author of this poetry has always tried to make 3-dimensional decisions, he was acutely aware throughout how impossible it is to be able to please *all*.

What readers will have noticed, who have taken a look at any section of volume one of 'Book of Jesus', is that at the end of each section, the exact New Testament references have been provided for each of the gospel passages (in some cases a single source) on which that verse translation has been based. This makes it easy, for those who are interested, to refer back to the actual gospels - in whichever translation they please. What it is important to emphasize at this point is that, even though each chapter has been intimately based on the source texts, this is, as a work of poetry, an *artistic production*. As such, after all "due diligence" was exercised in regard to any passage, a certain degree of 'poetic license' was taken, and the composer of this translation must avow **all errors** *are his own.*

What the current translator has aimed to do throughout the composition of this unified version of the New Testament gospels in verse, has been to try and see every single event of the gospels with *new eyes* and to hear every single word of them with *new ears.* As historical documents, each of the gospels has been treated with the gravity that they deserve, and on no occasion have any verses been rushed into existence without ensuring that they were as close as possible to their sources. At the same time, the writer has made the utmost effort to conduct this translation in an objective way: not as a Christian, not as an atheist, but rather in the spirit of one who has not made up their mind — so an *agnostic, non-believer, non-faith* perspective, if you like. One reason for this is that I wish the text to speak for itself and to be wary of adding attitude or opinion to what is translated. As there are *four true authors* of this work, it is **their** *voices* that must be heard. It is true that as multiple voices are fused into one voice in the case of many passages, it can be impossible to identify whose voice is speaking. However, I believe *unity in the account of events* is more important than any particular voice.

The reason why this work is composed in poetry, is because I became aware that no balanced gospel harmony in verse, in line with the most up-to-date New Testament research, existed in modern English. The few attempts that I could find were in asinine rhyme or set in poetic forms (such as the sonnet) that are unsuited to bible text. Poetry has an ability to bring scenes to life in way that prose can rarely achieve, and once I proved to myself that it was *possible* to express gospel words in modern English verse, I was committed to translating the whole in the same manner. What I found more than anything else in the writing of this book, is that Jesus *is a poet*, both in the way he expresses his ideas and as a master storyteller. He uses words in a way that makes them wield power, and I discovered at every turn, that not only his words but the gospel narrative as a whole, were supremely suited to poetry.

    When I approached this task, it was with the intention of ensuring that even though this version of the gospels is in verse, and unified in a single, mostly chronological narrative, it should not for that reason be weak in terms of its textual research or of a lower level of accuracy than if it were in prose. Additionally, I came to this challenge with the aim of making sure that the language used should not only be as close as possible to the gospel sources, but also as *experiential* as possible. The language of Jesus himself has many facets, and I wanted to try and embrace all of these. He speaks as a wise teacher, as a compassionate healer and a rousing activist, to mention just three of his voices. He uses words as his weapon of peace, and with him his words are actions in themselves, through which he speaks **to** the people and **for** the people, giving them new belief with his words and giving them new voices with which to express themselves. The 'Good News' he shares is something that he wants his followers to continuing sharing, so he does so with words so powerful in their poetry that they would go on to spread around the entire world. It is a hope of the author of this translation, that its poetry may go some distance toward doing justice to the words of the four gospels. —

I make all the foregoing comments in the spirit of an APOLOGY, for the task that I have undertaken is not perhaps a natural or necessary one to embark upon, even though *to me* it seemed to be one that I was meant to undertake, a task that I felt fully compelled to complete, no matter what might be its results — which it is **entirely** *up to the reader to decide*. Although this work was suggested by the publishers, no-one in any way necessitated the existence of this unified verse translation of the gospels. It is only a task that the author has *felt* obliged to pursue, at no-one else's compulsion — including that of the publishers. At the same time, the author *also felt* as if there were a perpetual requirement laying upon him to explain himself: give reasons **why** he has written this book. As a single human being I sense nothing more persistently than the pressentiment that what I have produced may be so wholly misguided *as I have failed to take notice of the hole I have dug myself into* — the prospect of producing a verse translation of the four New Testament gospels into modern English verse that does justice to the language and individuality of each of the four gospels: ***an impossible aim to achieve***. It would be absurd to assume that I have accomplished this in any way whatsoever. It is not, in my opinion, a "doable task", but something like the multiplication by itself of the *non-achievable* **7** tasks of Hercules into its square number, of **49** *even more unattainable aims!* — However, **that** is not what I set out to achieve. This volume now behind me, the avenues of research exhausted that I felt necessary to its writing, I only hope that this new verse translation of the gospels will be a positive reading experience *qua* poetical biography of Jesus.

A UNIFIED GOSPEL IN ENGLISH VERSE

# BOOK of JESUS

## VOLUME II

**OUT DECEMBER 2025**

www.bookofjes.us

BEFORE
*All Else*
existed,

*Logos*
WAS

- the Word
which WAS
with GOD

and which
*itself*
WAS **GOD**.

Published by

This Publication is set in
**Gloucester MT Extra Condensed** and
Adobe Devangarari

*Whoever does EVIL despises the LIGHT and evades its glare for **fear** their deeds will be exposed;*

*but those who live their lives through TRUTH shall enter in the LIGHT, that all may see what they have done within the EYES of GOD.*

JESUS OF NAZARETH

www.ingramcontent.com/pod-product-compliance
Lightning Source LLC
Chambersburg PA
CBHW042047280426
43661CB00120B/1493/J